Housing and Planning in the Countryside

GEOGRAPHY AND PUBLIC POLICY RESEARCH STUDIES SERIES

Series Editor: **Dr. John Whitelegg**
Department of Geography, University of Lancaster, England

1. A Spatial Analysis of Urban Community Development Policy in India
   Derek R. Hall

2. Housing and Planning in the Countryside
   G. Clark

Housing and Planning in the Countryside

Gordon

G. Clark, M.A.,Ph.D.
Department of Geography, University of Lancaster, England

RESEARCH STUDIES PRESS
A DIVISION OF JOHN WILEY & SONS LTD.
Chichester · New York · Brisbane · Toronto · Singapore

RESEARCH STUDIES PRESS

Editorial Office:
58B Station Road, Letchworth, Herts. SG6 3BE, England

Library of Congress Cataloguing in Publication Data:

Clark, G. (Gordon), 1950–
   Housing and planning in the countryside.
   Bibliography: p.
   Includes index.
   1. Housing, Rural—Great Britain.   2. Land use,
   Rural—Great Britain—Planning.   I. Title.
   HD7289.G8C58   363.5'0941   82-292
   ISBN 0 471 10212 1   AACR2

British Library Cataloguing in Publication Data:

Clark, G.
   Housing and planning in the countryside.
   (Geography and public policy research studies
   series; v.2)
   1. Housing—Great Britain
   I. Title   II. Series
   363.5'0941   HD7289.G7

   ISBN 0 471 10212 1

Printed in Great Britain

To my parents

Acknowledgements

I would like to acknowledge the assistance of Miss Maureen Boyd, the research assistant for the project funded by the Lake District Special Planning Board on which this book is based. Mr. Robert Forster and Mrs. Margaret Capstick also provided invaluable help and advice during the project.

I would also like to thank Mrs. Anne Jackson and Mr. Peter Mingins who drew the maps and Miss Dawn Phazey and Mrs. Jean Burford who typed the book.

The series editor, Dr. John Whitelegg, provided much valuable guidance for which I am very grateful.

Table of Contents

1. Introduction 1
2. Changing themes 5
3. Current issues in housing and
   planning 29
4. Housing and planning in the
   Lake District 49
5. Alternative housing strategies .. 111
6. Conflicts in rural planning 137
   Bibliography 151
   Index 157

List of Tables

Table 1. Urban and rural housing conditions in Scotland, 1971 26

Table 2. Cottage provision by occupation of worker, 1971-3 34

Table 3. Average gross weekly earnings, 1974 62

Table 4. Activity rates 62

Table 5. Size of waiting lists for council houses 62

Table 6. Current parish of residence and desired parish for households on waiting lists 65-6

Table 7. Building rates: dwellings completed (1967-74) per 1,000 population 69

Table 8. Status and current housing of households on waiting lists 69

Table 9. Present addresses of applicants living outside the National Park 71

Table 10. Major reasons for households being on waiting lists 72

Table 11. First preference of Allerdale applicants for a council house 75

Table 12. Status and current housing of households leaving Allerdale waiting list, March 1979 to March 1980 77

Table 13. Reasons for leaving
           waiting list for council
           house in Allerdale 77

Table 14. Households' reasons for
           leaving waiting list
           and their housing
           points 79

Table 15. Households' reasons for
           leaving waiting list and
           their period on waiting
           list 80

Table 16. Length of time on waiting
           list and points score 83

Table 17. Households lacking one
           or more standard house-
           hold amenities 85

Table 18. Status at February 1980
           of houses approved
           between September 1977
           and June 1979 101

Table 19. Comparative house
           prices 101

Table 20. Definitions of 'local'
           in Section 52
           agreements 106

Table 21. Household amenities in
           1971 in Western Isles
           and Scotland 118

Table 22. Distribution of sub-
           standard houses and
           housing grants in the
           Western Isles 119

Table 23. Crofters' housing
           grants after 1976 119

List of Illustrations

Figure   1   Howard's Three
              Magnets 13

Figure   2   Forest villages in
              Northumberland 15

Figure   3   Agricultural smallholdings
              in Scotland 17

Figure   4   Tied cottages in
              Great Britain, 1972-3 33

Figure   5   The Lake District 50

Figure   6   Settlement pattern in the
              Lake District 52

Figure   7   Functional areas in
              Cumbria - pattern of
              shopping in 1971 54

Figure   8   Landownership in the
              Lake District 56

Figure   9   The 1936 afforestation
              agreement in the Lake
              District 58

Figure 10   Forest and woodland
              policy in the Lake
              District National Park 59

Figure 11   Estimated mean house-
              hold income in Cumbria 61

Figure 12   Number of council
              houses in the Lake
              District National
              Park 68

Figure 13   Council housing and
              waiting lists in the
              Lake District National
              Park 74

Figure 14   Housing stress in
              Cumbria 76

Figure 15   House building in
             Cumbria, 1967-74   82

Figure 16   Private house building
             by district, 1967-74   82

Figure 17   Improvement grants in
             Cumbria, 1968-74   84

Figure 18   Population change by
             parish, 1951-71   86

Figure 19   Population structure by
             parish, 1961-71   87

Figure 20   Expansion of
             Braithwaite village,
             Cumbria   89

Figure 21   House prices in South
             Lakeland District   90

Figure 22   Advertisements for
             houses, cottages and
             flats in Cumbria,
             1981   92-4

Figure 23   Second homes by parish
             in the Lake District
             National Park   95

Figure 24   Distribution of completed
             Section 52
             agreements   100

Figure 25   Completed Section 52
             houses, August 1980   102

Figure 26   Crofters' common
             grazings in Scotland   113

Figure 27   Landownership units in
             the Western Isles in
             ca. 1970   115

Figure 28   Population trends in
             the Western Isles,
             1801-1971   117

Figure 29   House prices in the
             Isle of Man,
             1965-79   122

Figure 30   New dwellings completed
             in the Isle of Man,
             1972-9 124

Figure 31   Mortgage repayments as a
             proportion of income
             given different rates
             of income inflation 133

Figure 32   Types of rural area
             in England and Wales 135

1. Introduction

Progress, therefore, is not an accident, but a necessity.

It is a part of nature.

                                      H. Spencer Social Statics (1850)

What is a house? To the person living in it, a house is a home but to an architect it is a commission, perhaps a chance to be original or just another job. To a landlord it may be a financial liability or a valuable supplementary pension, while a local authority will see it as a commitment to public expenditure on roads and services. Housing means many things to different people since so many have an interest in whether it is constructed, how and where it is built, and who resides in it. This simple observation is one of the starting points for this study.

Another is the cost of housing. For most people who buy a house, it is probably the biggest purchase they will ever make in their lives. Whether they have a mortgage or are tenants, the resulting periodic payments for the house can represent a considerable outgoing. Houses are expensive. They also represent a large proportion of the personal wealth of most of their owners. In 1980 houses and land represented 26 per cent of the personal sector's assets in the U.S.A. compared with only 19 per cent in 1965. In the United Kingdom housing represented 42 per cent of the estimated personal assets of households in 1980 (The Economist, 5 September 1981 p.54). Selling a house has become one of the few legal ways of making a capital gain which is not taxed. The building societies which have financed the rising trend to owner-occupation in Britain have grown until in 1976 they accounted for 17.8 per cent of British households' financial assets. Forty-three per cent of British adults now invest with a building society (Boddy, 1980 p.42) and they account for 47 per cent of personal sector deposits (The Economist, 19 September 1981 p.16). Housing is big business based on small savings.

Housing also has a deep social significance. Shelter and warmth are basic human needs but a house is more than just the means of meeting these requirements. It can represent social status by its location, size and style. A family's housing requirements change with time and circumstances. Houses should ideally adapt to these changes, but of course this does not always happen. Overcrowding, or a widow alone in a five-bedroomed house are the results. Everyone needs housing but few can build their own house. A house of any comfort needs land and materials not found lying around as well as special skills and the time to construct it. Generally the labour, materials and skills have to be obtained from someone else and the terms on which they are made available is the root cause of many of the features of housing we can observe today. The interests of the land-owners and builders may not coincide with those of the potential householders. That is one reason why government has become involved in housing, regulating tenancies between private individuals and providing financial support for public and private housing. As always the introduction of public policy, which is also party policy, into so multi-faceted and essential an area as housing creates new tensions and contradictions while at the same time resolving others.

Yet government action cannot alter the basic facts of housing. People aspire to certain types of house as well as simply needing a house - housing is not a homogenous commodity but a highly differentiated and expensive product. Therefore circumstances may arise allowing a less than perfect market to develop - indeed some, such as Harvey, would go further and argue that all housing is, to a greater or lesser extent, an individual or class monopoly. How different groups react to such a situation when it arises is another theme which will be explored in this study. However, this book is not about housing in general. It is about the relatively **under-research**ed area of houses in rural areas and this restriction brings to our attention an additional set of preconceptions, images and myths distinctive to the countryside. In the nineteenth century, rural housing, like many rural matters, figured prominently in the work of Royal Commissions, party politics and the outpourings of polemicists. The countryside has become less of a problem because it is smaller in area and population than before. Perhaps correctly, urban housing has been the focus of attention for a hundred years. The assumption that rural areas either do not share the problems of urban housing or are not interesting areas in their own right in which to study housing, needs to be firmly refuted. Housing in rural areas can be as idyllic or as obnoxious as in the city. The influence of govern-ment policies and of competing private interests are as worthy of study in rural areas as anywhere else and, arguably, are more important because of the lack of choice inherent in areas of low population density. Since there are fewer houses, local authorities and industries and also fewer owners of land and houses, the actions of each became individually more important in determining the overall housing situation in a country area.

The book will initially review the development of rural housing principally in the United Kingdom during the last century since it is in this period that the origins of today's housing problems can be found (Chapter 2). The quality of rural housing, as with urban housing, has improved immeasurably since then but the problematic relationship between housing and employment and between housing and the public interest were as complex then as now (Chapter 3). These issues will be explored more thoroughly in their modern context with particular reference to the Lake District in north-west England (Chapter 4). This area is a microcosm of many of the pressures and conflicts to be found in the countryside - the shortage of the right houses in the right locations, the arrival of urban newcomers, the effect on housing of the structural changes in the economy and the increase in personal mobility. All these are set within the institutional framework of a National Park and the curiously distinctive system of rural land-use planning in Great Britain. Simultaneously, successive national governments have implemented agricultural and fiscal policies, amongst others, which were not intended to affect rural housing but demonstrably have done so. The intended and the unforeseen effects of planning action will be examined in the Lake District to illuminate broader features of the interaction between rural housing and planning in Great Britain. In Chapter 5 some alternative strategies for dealing with the distinctive housing problems in areas such as the Lake District will be examined drawing on the experience of other rural areas.

Finally, some conclusions will be drawn on the future directions of rural housing provision and on its relationship with rural planning. Inevitably this will reunite rural housing with many other aspects of the countryside from which it can only be separated briefly for descriptive convenience. There is a reflexive relationship between housing, economy and society. Housing is partly a reflection of the other two as they were in the past - a palimpsest of old relationships reinterpreted uneasily under modern conditions. Housing is also a catalyst of change - the place where wider conflicts are resolved and the spark which fires off other changes in rural communities. For these reasons alone, the geography of rural Britain cannot be understood without a concern for housing.

2. Changing Themes

'It is my belief, Watson, founded upon my experience, that the
lowest and vilest alleys of London do not present a more dreadful
record of sin than does the smiling and beautiful countryside.'
                Sir Arthur Conan Doyle The Copper Beeches (1892).

The task is still the same - to bring the stock of houses nearer the
aspirations of those living in the countryside and of those in the
towns who would like to join them. What has changed is the way the
mismatch between reality and the ideal is perceived. What specifically is wrong with the housing? Is it the number of houses or their
quality that is deficient or is it their cost, tenure, appearance or
their location? All these features of rural houses have been
criticised as deficient at some time during the last 150 years.
Similarly, the aggrieved party has changed too. Who precisely is
discomfited by this deficiency in the housing? It is not always the
inhabitant of the substandard house who is seen as the loser because
of its less than perfect character. The preferred solution to the
deficiency in the housing stock has also changed. The solution may
be to demolish the house and re-house the occupants or it may be to
improve the house or it may involve letting someone else occupy the
house. The solution may require philanthropy, Smith's 'invisible
hand', private enterprise or public subsidy. Housing people is still
the aim and it has always constituted a problem for some group in
society. What has changed is the way that task is structured and
perceived and how different interest groups have manoeuvred to
secure the acceptance of their definition of the problem and their
solution.

2.1 EARLY DEVELOPMENTS

It is difficult to generalise about rural housing for all the
groups in the countryside and the considerable regional variations in
conditions. By the early nineteenth century the practice of boarding
single farm labourers in the farmer's house was becoming obsolete in
much of England. However in northern England and south-east Scotland
it continued throughout the century and, on a small-scale, until
after the Second World War. All the farm labourers ate together in
the farmhouse kitchen under this system and the workers slept in the
'chaumer' - an area set aside for them in the loft or above the
stables. The system fell victim to the growing social distance felt
between farmer and labourer and also its demise was hastened by the
decline in the number of farm workers as the nineteenth century passed.

In south-east Scotland there was another group of farm workers - the hinds - who came to be specialist labourers particularly for ploughing. Their living conditions were much better since they rented a smallholding and a cottage near the farmstead. The hind and his wife employed a bondager - a female helper - to work both for them and the farm, which reproduced, at a lower level in the emerging social hierarchy, the relationship between labourers and farmer (Whittington). In east-central and north-east Scotland there was an alternative system of housing ploughmen and labourers in bothies. These were separate buildings where the workers lived together and cooked for themselves, again in rather poor conditions. Even when they married, the farm labourers often lived apart from their wives for most of the week. Only the fear of all the workers leaving the farm at one of the twice-yearly markets for hiring labour acted to keep conditions from deteriorating too far. It would be tempting to attribute poor housing to all farm workers but this would be to ignore both the social stratification and differences in earnings among the groups within the labourers and the considerable regional variations in their conditions of service.

As the nineteenth century progressed these kitchen and bothy systems were replaced by a more recognisably modern custom of labourers 'living out'. They either rented a cottage as tenants-at-will often from the farmer who employed them or they had use of a cottage 'free', that is, their wages were reduced by the amount of rent they would have paid. They could therefore be simultaneously dismissed and evicted, yet this real vulnerability was not identi-fied by contemporary commentators as the principal problem. The concern regarding farm workers' cottages focussed primarily on the poor quality of the house usually as a symptom of their general poverty. Evidence, both anecdotal and statistical, for this concern was displayed by all sides.

'The Irish people is thus held in crushing poverty, from which it cannot free itself under our present social conditions. These people live in the most wretched clay huts, scarcely good enough for cattle-pens, have scant food all winter long, or, as the report above quoted expresses it, they have potatoes half enough thirty weeks in the year, and the rest of the year nothing. When the time comes in the spring at which this provision reaches its end, or can no longer be used because of its sprouting, wife and children go forth to beg and tramp the country with their kettle in their hands. Meanwhile the husband, after planting potatoes for the next year, goes in search of work either in Ireland or England, and returns at the potato harvest to his family. This is the condition in which nine-tenths of the Irish country folks live. They are poor as church mice, wear the most wretched rags, and stand upon the lowest plane of intelligence possible in a half-civilised country'

(Engels, 1892 p.272).

Samuel Johnson's powers of observation were more acute since he identified at least two social groups in the Scottish Hebrides in

1773 on the basis of their types of house.

'The habitations of men in the Hebrides may be distinguished
into huts and houses. By a "house," I mean a building with one
storey over another; by a "hut," a dwelling with only one floor.
The laird, who formerly lived in a castle, now lives in a house;
sometimes sufficiently neat, but seldom very spacious or
splendid. The tacksmen and the ministers have commonly houses.
Wherever there is a house, the stranger finds a welcome, and to
the other evils of exterminating tacksmen may be added the
unavoidable cessation of hospitality, of the devolution of too
heavy a burden on the ministers.

Of the houses little can be said. They are small, and by the
necessity of accumulating stores, where there are so few
opportunities of purchase, the rooms are very heterogeneously
filled. With want of cleanliness it were ingratitude to
reproach them. The servants having been bred upon the naked
earth, think every floor clean, and the quick succession of
guests, perhaps not always over-elegant, does not allow much time
for adjusting their apartments.

Huts are of many gradations; from murky dens to commodious
dwellings'

(Johnson, 1971 pp.99-100).

As an Englishman, Johnson was echoing a frequent comment by
travellers in Scotland when he viewed housing as generally of a very
low standard north of the Border. Writing of the sixteenth and
seventeenth centuries Whyte noted some cases in point.

'One thing which all English travellers in seventeenth-century
Scotland agreed upon was the poor standard of rural housing.
They criticised the lowness of the houses, the absence of
chimneys and windows, the generally poor construction, and the
accommodation of men and beasts in close proximity under one
roof.

When Martin Frobisher's expedition called at Orkney in 1577,
outward bound for the North-West Passage, the primitive dwellings
of the inhabitants excited almost as much interest as those of
the Eskimoes of Baffin Island: 'their houses are very simply
builded with pebble stone, without any chimneys, the fire being
made in the midst thereof. The good man, wife, children and
other of their family eat and sleep on one side of the house and
the cattle on the other, very beastly and rudely in respect of
civility.' Seventy years later, a Cromwellian soldier described
Lowland houses as being 'low thatcht cottages full of smoke and
noysome smells: in many places their families and cattell be under
one roof.' There did not appear to be much difference in basic
housing standards throughout the country.'

(Whyte, 1979 p.162-3).

Such judgements were not confined to either Scotland or the pre-nineteenth century period as Cobbett showed in some of the more indignant passages of his Rural Rides. He wrote scathingly of some houses he saw in Leicestershire in 1832.

'Look at the miserable sheds in which the labourers reside!
Look at these hovels, made of mud and of straw; bits of glass,
or of old, off-cast windows, without frames or hinges frequently,
but merely stuck in the mud wall. Enter them, and look at the
bits of chairs or stools; the wretched boards tacked together
to serve for a table; the floor of pebble, broken brick, or of
the bare ground; look at the thing called a bed; and survey the
rags on the backs of the wretched inhabitants; and then wonder
if you can that the gaols and dungeons and treadmills increase,
and that a standing army and barracks are become the favourite
establishments of England!'

(Cobbett, 1967 p.266).

Sixty years later the politically more moderate Labour Commission of 1892-4 noted only some improvement in general housing standards in the English countryside with less over-crowding but conditions were still lamentable.

'The supply of cottages is not now generally defective in
respect of numbers, owing partly to the decrease in the rural
population and partly to the large number of cottages which
have been built by large landowners and others who can afford to
build without an expectation of a profitable return for their
outlay...

The distribution of cottages is irregular, and their situation
often very inconvenient for the inhabitants...

The accommodation provided in respect of the number, size and
comfort of the rooms, the sanitary condition and the water
supply are lamentably deficient generally, and require amend-
ment...

The rent has generally no relation to the size of the cottage,
the cost of its construction, the accommodation which it affords,
its condition as regards repair or sanitary arrangements, or to
the earnings of the occupant...'

(Burnett, 1978 p.132).

The developing medical lobby of the second half of the nineteenth century drew attention to the consequences of such housing for the health of the occupants. In 1876 Edward Smith articulated this concern simply and clearly.

'A man may carry his rheumatism, acquired from the sweating walls
and 'heaving' floor of his ruinous dwelling, to a good old age;
the peasant, gaining immunity from his open-air existence, may

escape the noxious results of stagnant drains, and even of impure
water; but it is his sleeping accommodation which produces the
most insidious (and often fatal) results upon his health.
Overcrowding has probably killed more than all other evil
conditions whatever.'

(Burnett, 1978 p.44).

Overcrowding was a concern from a medical point of view and it also
provoked decided views on other different grounds as the Rector of
Blandford in Dorest noted.

'I do not choose to put on paper the disgusting scenes that I
have known to occur from this promiscuous crowding of the sexes
together. Seeing, however, to what the mind of the young female
is exposed from her very childhood, I have long ceased to wonder
at the otherwise seeming precocious licentiousness of conversation
which may be heard in every field where many of the young are
at work together.'

(Burnett, 1978 p.45).

Whether one examines the writings of radicals like Cobbett and
Engels or Government reports, one notices how consistently observers
identified the physical state of the poorest rural housing as the
principal evil. What was needed was self-evidently dry floors, the
removal of livestock from the same building as the people and
weatherproof roofs and walls of solid construction with controlled
ventilation for the removal of smoke and the prevention of miasma.
Miasma was the term given to stagnant fetid air in houses which was
believed by many doctors in the mid-nineteenth century to cause
disease. Other observers were more concerned with the medical consequences of poor housing - the rheumatism from the damp floors, the
contaminated water supply and the prevalence of infections induced by
a lack of cleanliness. This group viewed the poor housing as only one
part of the problem which also included poor nutrition and lack of
personal hygiene. Lack of information and poverty were the root
causes and poor housing just one symptom of this. A third group
identified the real difficulty as the small size rather than the poor
construction of the houses since this led to overcrowding and worse.
The high rates of illegitimacy in some rural areas were invariably
ascribed to overcrowding (or navvies building the railways) while the
generally uncongenial surroundings of much rural housing were said to
drive men into public houses. The resulting drunkenness was held
responsible for vandalism, assault and rowdy behaviour. An enquiry
in 1864 into housing conditions in 1851 showed that over half the
cottages in 821 parishes had fewer than two bedrooms and, given large
families, the cottages had only 62.5 per cent of the minimum air
space recommended for common lodging houses (Burnett, 1978 p.43). By
1900 overcrowding was not so acute a problem as earlier in the century
due to urban migration, reduced family size and some new cottage
building but, as will be seen, there was still considerable cause for
concern.

Some observers were more perceptive and noted that although poverty
was associated with poor housing, many labouring families could
afford to spend more than they did on housing when times were good.
However, continuity of employment could not always be guaranteed
particularly in arable areas and it was the likelihood of having to
to survive periods of illness or bad weather on low earnings that
restricted farm workers to renting the poorest of housing. Similarly,
some labourers were able to afford better housing in their middle
years when most of their children were earning. Earlier in their
married life, and later when illness and infirmity took their toll,
greater poverty was normal and the poorest housing was all they could
afford. The situation had been worsened by the Poor Law and enclosure which tended to reduce the number of rural cottages. Prior to
the Union Chargeability Act of 1865 some landowners pulled down
cottages forcing people to move to other parishes. If they then
became a charge on the Poor Law funds, other landowners would have to
pay for them.

There was an indifference to housing improvement from both local
and national government and yet improvements did take place.
Enlightened landowners such as the Duke of Bedford built houses for
their workers though opinions differed on whether this could ever be
profitable. The Bedford estates used standardised designs and
specialist building squads and claimed to obtain a three per cent
return on houses in the mid-nineteenth century but by 1885 inflated
building costs had reduced this to one half per cent (Burnett, 1978
p.133). Others claimed that the cost of even a £60 cottage would
never be recouped from rents in under fifteen years. Certainly very
few landowners or others built speculative housing for farm workers
which points to the inherent unprofitability of renting housing to
the lowest paid farm workers when compared with the eight or ten per
cent return normally sought at that time by investors in real property.
In 1913 Rowntree found only five counties, all in northern England,
where average farm wages were high enough to provide the average size
of family with acceptable accommodation. There was a movement to
build model cottages such as Hardwick village (Nottinghamshire) which
was built in flamboyant style by the Dukes of Newcastle, but this did
little except set standards which only unstinting philanthropy or
public subsidy could attain. Neither source of finance was large
enough before 1914 to improve rural housing nationally.

There were some who dismissed the need for housing improvement.
They pointed to the many good houses for farmers, the craftsmen of the
community and the better-paid farm workers (a few of whom owned the
freehold of their cottages). There had also been a steady rate of
new house building in the countryside - about 9000 houses a year
between 1841 and 1891 in England and Wales. The rate of new house
construction increased in the last quarter of the nineteenth century
but much of this was suburban rather than truly rural (Rogers, 1976
p.87). They also advanced 'coal-in-the-bath' arguments such as that
thatched roofs improved the ventilation and extra bedrooms would only
be used to keep the pigs. By the end of the nineteenth century such

progress as there had been on improving housing had relied on
philanthropy, continued urban migration, smaller families, some model
estates, a more prosperous agriculture (particularly in horticulture
and dairying), equalisation of the poor rate and, after 1865, the
opportunity to borrow from the Enclosure Commissioners for cottage
improvement. Together these did improve the situation but grounds for
concern still existed. Statistical evidence on changes in the quality
of rural housing is not available but the declining rural population
was very important in relieving overcrowding. The prospect of a job
in the cities or the Empire was probably a more powerful stimulus to
migration than poor housing. By 1906, 91 per cent of the Glasgow
police force were born in the countryside and so were 66 per cent of
the Metropolitan Police. A realisation was dawning that the way to
improve rural housing was not through philanthropy, though this could
make a contribution, nor was it by complicated Housing Acts such as
those of 1890 and 1909 which were financially and administratively
unworkable. Local authority housing attracted some commentators but
its general acceptance was slow and by 1914 only 1 per cent of the
national housing stock was publicly owned compared with 10 per cent
owner-occupied and 80 per cent privately rented (Boddy, 1980 p.154).
Most of the publicly owned housing was in the major cities such as
Liverpool, London and Glasgow. Some objected to local authority
housing as simply a subsidy to farmers who were relieved the cost of
providing housing themselves and who could pay lower wages.

2.2 CONFRONTING THE ISSUE?

For the believer in the efficiency and equity of the free market,
progress towards better housing would come through the better-off
buying new houses and vacating their old houses for those less well
paid. The poorest quality houses would become surplus to requirements
and should be demolished. For those sceptical of the freedom of the
free market, improved housing could come in one of three ways. The
first was the building of completely new settlements, the second was
to provide conditions which would encourage rural employers to build
houses for their workers and bear the loss and the third was for a
programme of centrally-funded house building.

The first of these reactions to the poverty of some rural houses
was to turn one's back on the countryside and look to garden cities
as a better alternative to urban migration. Migration was often seen
as inevitable given the depressed state of some sectors of farming
between 1875 and 1914 but the scale of that migration was thought to
have been increased by, among other things, the poor housing in the
countryside. There was no way rural housing could be improved
according to this view and stopping or reducing urban migration was
seen as imperative. Farming was losing its labour force and the
overcrowded cities could accept no more people. The best known
advocate of a middle way between rural slum and urban slum was
Ebenezer Howard through his exposition of the Garden City in 1898.
This desire for an idealist solution can be traced back at least as
far as Robert Owen's New Lanark in the early nineteenth century and it

can also be seen in the communities set up particularly in America by
religious groups such as the Hutterites, Mennonites, Shakers and
Mormons. The principal inspiration for the Garden City movement was
as much the awfulness of the city as the poverty of the countryside.
Lord Rosebery, the Chairman of London County Council made the point
clearly in 1891.

'There is no thought of pride associated in my mind with the idea
of London. I am always haunted by the awfulness of London: by
the great appalling fact of these millions cast down, as it would
appear by hazard, on the banks of this noble stream working each
in their own groove and their own cell, without regard or knowledge of each other, without heeding each other, without having
the slightest idea how the other lives - the heedless casualty of
of unnumbered thousands of men. Sixty years ago a great Englishman, Cobbett, called it a wen. If it was a wen then, what is it
now? A tumour, an elephantiasis sucking into its gorged system
half the life and the blood and the bone of the rural districts.'
(Howard, 1946 p.42).

Sending the migrants back to the countryside, as Sir John Gorst
suggested in 1891 - 'they must back the tide, and stop the migration
of the people into the towns' - was clearly not practicable (Howard,
1946 p.42). Howard's analogy of magnets with their repelling and
attracting poles saw the poor housing and sanitary arrangements of
rural houses as among the features promoting urban migration (Figure
1). Yet the proposal for new towns was most deficient with respect to
the central issue of housing. The Garden City which Howard envisaged
was clearly superior to town or country in terms of housing density
and in the provision of parks, infrastructure and cultural facilities,
but the proposals for housing were tentative and vague. Unlike much
else, the housing was to be provided privately by enlightened landlords. 'The municipality would be attempting too much if it essayed
this task (housing provision) at least at the outset' (Howard, 1946
p.106). The municipal authority could help by lowering housing
densities - would this not tend to raise rents? - and by providing
construction sites at a lower rent than otherwise - an indirect subsidy. The basic profitability for landlords under Howard's scheme of
speculative housing for rent to the low paid remains in doubt therefore and largely untested except in the garden cities of Letchworth
(1903) and Welwyn Garden City (1920) which Howard started. By the
time the Garden City had been transformed into the centrally-financed
new towns in the late 1940s, their contribution to the housing of the
specifically rural population had become insignificant.

The second reaction to poor houses was that rural employers should
build their own houses. Again the undercurrent of holding on to
workers can be detected as strongly as any simple desire to provide
better houses. However, building houses was not popular since the
arable farmers of eastern Britain, who employed the most hired labour,
were the most depressed sector of British agriculture up to 1914.
Blythe recorded the effects of this depression in 'Akenfield'.

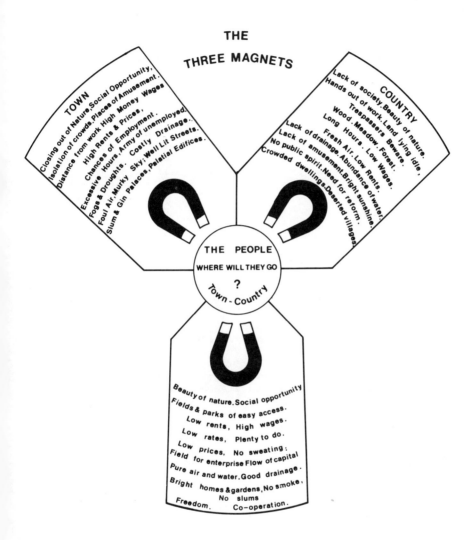

FIG.1.   Howard's Three Magnets (after Howard, 1946).

'Very soon after this (about 1905) it was very hard living indeed
for the family. There were seven children at home and father's
wages had been reduced to 10s. a week. Our cottage was nearly
empty - except for people. There was a scrubbed brick floor and
just one rug made of scraps of old clothes pegged into a sack.
The cottage had a living-room, a larder and two bedrooms. Six of
us boys and girls slept in one bedroom and our parents and the
baby slept in the other. There was no newspaper and nothing to
read except the Bible. All the village houses were like this.

Our food was apples, potatoes, swedes and bread, and we drank our
tea without milk or sugar. Skim milk could be bought from the
farm but it was thought a luxury. Nobody could get enough to eat
no matter how they tried. Two of my brothers were out of work.
One was eight years old and he got 3s. a week, the other got about
7s. Our biggest trouble was water. There was no water near, it
all had to be fetched from the foot of a hill nearly a mile away.
'Drink all you can at school', we were told - there was a tap at
school.'

(Blythe, 1969 pp.34-5).

Even after the First World War, the easy profits of the war years
were short-lived and in 1921 the withdrawal of subsidies reduced
farm incomes and started a new period of low incomes for farmers and
farm workers which was only modestly relieved in the arable areas by
the subsidies on cereals, ploughing and lime in the 1930s. The
farmers did not have much money with which to build new houses or
renovate the old ones.

One of the few expanding rural employers which did have enough money
was the Forestry Commission. This had been established in 1919 to
provide a strategic reserve of timber for Britain in time of war. The
Commission soon found itself operating in areas remote from existing
settlements and decided to reduce the cost to its employees of
travelling to their work by building new villages for them near to the
forests. In the areas where they were operating, the existing stock
of often isolated houses could not house all their workers even after
renovation. In Northumberland in north-east England there was some
opposition to new villages from the County Council which preferred
the expansion of existing settlements. When the forestry programme
was expanded after 1945, five forestry villages were established in
the county with others in central Wales, south-west Scotland and
Argyllshire (Figure 2). The physical standard of the housing was as
good as the post-war years allowed and certainly they have retained
small populations in rural areas - the five Northumberland villages
comprised a total of 234 houses in 1972 (Smith, 1976 p.4). However
they have had their critics who complained not only of the teething
troubles inherent in any new settlement (high staff turnover, for
example) but also of the one-class character of the villages where
everyone earned similar wages and worked for the same employer.
The isolation and a lack of social facilities contingent on the
village's small size have raised the cost of living there since a car
(75 per cent of families had one despite low wages) or an expensive

15

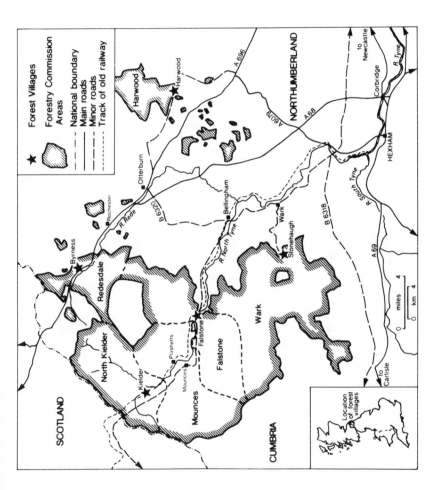

FIG.2. Forest villages in Northumberland (after Smith, 1976).

bus journey is needed for most shopping or entertainment journeys.
This sense of isolation was made more stark for some of the workers
in north-east England and Wales because nearly half came from towns
or colliery settlements and they found the contrast with a small,
isolated village severe. However the majority of those who were
surveyed by Smith in Northumberland had come to like the area and
nearly two-thirds had been living there for ten years or more and were
happy with their house and job. Despite everything, a sense of
community did develop in the forestry villages.

The cost of housing these people in the new villages was not only
higher for the people but also for the Forestry Commission who felt
duty bound to provide roads, village halls and churches as well as
houses. However, both the Commission and the workers saved on travel
costs to work. The irony is that the rapidly rising level of mechani-
sation in forestry had reduced the need for employees in the industry
far below the levels forecast on the basis of the technology of the
post-war years and one forestry village in Argyll has been completely
sold. The scale of provision was, of course, small, the Commission
owned only 2315 houses in the whole of Great Britain in 1979 and had
built only 2503 new houses between 1945 and 1965 as well as renovating
older houses (Ryle, 1969 p.196).

Of potentially greater numerical significance was the provision of
houses for crofters and smallholders in Britain after 1919. There
was no attempt here to create villages, just small farms and a loose
cluster of houses for the farmers. Built to a standard, rather suburban bungalow design, the scale of building often led to economies in
their construction. Smallholdings are a notable feature in many
European countries. In Denmark, 26,000 were created after legislation
in 1899 and 1919, in Norway 16,000 between 1921 and 1940 while
Finland and Italy also had active programmes (Mather, 1978 p.1). In
Scotland 450 forestry smallholdings were created, a few fishing
smallholdings were set up in Lewis and by 1955 nearly 3,400 agricultural smallholdings had been established in Scotland (Figure 3).
Also 1600 smallholdings were created on private estates in Scotland
using public finance (Mather, 1978 p.27). Most county councils in
England and Wales also set up smallholdings. Even though nearly all
had a house attached to them, the provision of housing was one of the
less important features of the policy except in Norway and Finland.
Smallholdings were primarily a means of creating jobs for the unemployed, the ex-serviceman or the refugee. Lloyd George's vision
was of three acres and a cow to keep families fed and provide the
first rung on a ladder to larger farms for the most skilled. It did
not work out that way since very few of the smallholders ever advanced
above that first rung. Smallholdings today are a liability for the
state since they are expensive to administer and the opportunity cost
of the capital locked up in the land is considerable. An active
programme of selling smallholdings is underway in several British
counties while elsewhere they are being amalgamated into units of a
size more suitable for the standard of living expected by farmers
today. Most smallholders also have other jobs, in agricultural con-

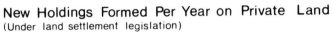

New Holdings Formed Per Year on Private Land
(Under land settlement legislation)

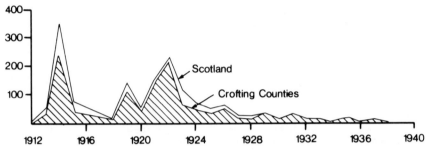

New Holdings Formed Per Year On Board/Department Of Agriculture Land

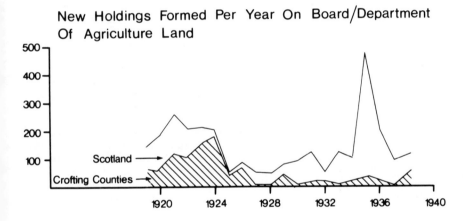

FIG.3.   Agricultural smallholdings in Scotland (after Mather, 1978).

tracting for example or in industry, the latter being particularly
common in West Germany. The smallholding is a difficult proposition
when seen as the sole means to an agricultural living but as a
contribution to the housing stock they had and still have a useful
role to play in the countryside.

The third method of improving rural housing conditions was by local
and central government building houses directly and letting them at a
rent the poorly paid could afford. While this course of action may
now seem obvious, it took a long time for the necessary political will
and financial aid to be collected. The problem had something of the
character of a Catch 22 situation. When there was a high proportion
of the population in poor rural houses, the scale of the problem was
too big to be tackled. Subsidy can only be given to small sectors
of society if an intolerable burden is not to be placed on the rest.
Yet when the proportion of the population in poor rural houses had
fallen very low, the scale of need in the cities was much greater and
more pressing. In addition, the cost of building houses in the
countryside is often higher than in towns - apart from London - since
the houses are often built in small numbers. In the more remote
parts of the country, they may take longer to build as the travelling
time of the work-force is greater. In addition the resources available to rural councils tend to be lower than in other areas. Thus a
penny on the rates in the Western Isles raises only £7000 since they
obtain £22 per head of population from the rates compared with £59 per
head in Scotland as a whole (Comhairle nan Eilean, 1976 p.65). Rural
authorities tend to be poor authorities and in the early days of this
century this lack of resources, for which central government then
made little systematic compensation, was the prime cause of the slow
take-up of the various schemes enacted for council-house building.

In 1912 the National Land and Home League canvassed the views of
local authorities on whether they could build houses for farm workers
without raising extra local revenue. Only 8 out of the 332 authorities which responded believed they could and predictably most
favoured centralised rather than local funding for any such programme
(Rogers, 1976 pp.86-7). Prior to 1914 only six per cent of all new
houses were built by local authorities and these were mostly in urban
areas. The inability, and indeed, unwillingness of rural authorities
even to conduct surveys of housing conditions, let alone build new
houses, was clearly demonstrated by the poor response to the Housing
Acts of 1890 and 1909. Swenarton has charted the conversion of
official housing policy from one of preventing crime and disease to
one, after 1919, of actually building houses for the lower paid as an
end in itself. He notes the importance of the garden city movement
as an exemplar for state housing and the fear of revolution, or at
least social unrest, as one of two spurs to overcome the Treasury and
Bank of England's abhorrence of public expenditure. The other was
to use taxpayers' money to supplement the rates in the embryonic slum
clearance schemes undertaken prior to 1914 by Conservative local
councils. In July 1914 the Liberal government introduced a Bill to
promote publicly funded rural housing as part of its reforming plat-
form. This was designed to build houses for better-off labourers

whose current housing, when vacated, would be occupied by the poorest
workers who had insanitary housing. The state of course would not
subsidise rents nor ensure a minimum wage which could meet economic
rents and so relied on this indirect approach with its assumption of
a process whereby people filtered up into better houses (Swenarton,
1981 p.41). Nonetheless by the outbreak of war in 1914 a consensus
on a mechanism for funding house building by public utility societies
had been agreed and only hostilities delayed its implementation. By
the end of the war when the Tudor Walters Report was published, the
state had decided that it should build houses directly rather than
fund societies to do it and the scale of the programme had increased
twenty-fold (Swenarton, 1981 p.47). The experience of housing large
numbers of people for expanded dockyards (eg Rosyth) and munitions
works (eg Woolwich Arsenal and at Gretna) had provided a model for
the 'homes-for-heroes' campaign even if the financial orthodoxy of
the period in the City delayed the practical execution of such a large
programme for many years.

The inter-war period was marked by a spate of legislation on housing
to which local authorities reacted with varying enthusiasm. Some
made use of the government subsidies available and built a considerable number of new houses while others, such as the Welsh authorities
were very lackadaisical. Between 1918 and 1939 no fewer than sixteen
Acts of Parliament dealing with English and Welsh housing were passed
along with ten Acts about rents and ten more were passed dealing
exclusively with housing in Scotland. In 1944 a committee estimated
that between 1919 and 1943 Rural District Councils had built nearly
160,000 new houses under these Acts while private enterprise had
built about 135,000 with subsidy (Rogers, 1976 p.93). In addition
County and District Councils had built nearly 5,000 houses without
subsidy and private builders had erected over 571,000 new unsubsidised
houses. Numerically, the total of over 870,000 new houses represented
an increase in the housing stock in rural areas of about 50 per cent
(Ministry of Works and Planning, 1942 p.23). The private enterprise
building was principally for owner-occupation and much of this was
essentially the suburban building characteristic of the sprawl of the
cities into nominally 'rural' districts. London, for example,
tripled its built-up area between the World Wars (Hall, 1974a p.34).
Most of the privately built houses which received subsidy (about 14
per cent of the total in England and Wales) did so under the 1923
Housing etc Act while the 1919 and 1924 Acts were the most effective
with the rural district councils since the subsidy for a rural house
was £3-10s. higher than for an urban one (Cullingworth, 1979 p.99).
At the end of the inter-war period, the 1938 Housing (Financial
Provisions) Act made specific provision for building houses for
agricultural workers (an early Act of 1926 was ineffective) but only
4,761 houses or 1.6 per cent of all the subsidised houses built
between the wars were built under this Act. If the Second World War
had not intervened its influence might have been much greater. The
1923 Act also helped private building by giving guarantees to building
societies which allowed them to raise the normal mortgage advance from
75 per cent of the house's valuation to 95 per cent.

Yet the effect of these measures was not great enough to solve the rural housing problem. For the low-paid farm worker with irregular wages, a council house would be too expensive - inter-war council houses were usually generously proportioned and economic rents were charged - and many farmers and rural authorities did not have enough money in the Depression to make their contribution to the new housing. This was particularly noticeable in Wales, East Anglia and south-west England (Rogers, 1976 p.90). A report on Rural Housing from the Scottish Housing Advisory Committee in 1937 noted much waste of public money on house improvements and the inability of rural counties to build houses for the general needs of workers. They often did not carry out surveys of their houses nor plan for their district, as required by Parliament. House improvement grants were not very popular since the owner of the house also had to contribute to the work but could not raise the rent above what an agricultural labourer could afford even though the house's assessment for rates would rise.

Nonetheless progress had been made. New houses had been built in the inter-war years at a rate unprecedented in the previous seventy years, 30,000 unfit houses had been demolished and 22,000 renovated (Rogers, 1976 p.92). This had been achieved by a concerted programme of subsidies to public and private builders starting in the mid-1920s with the expectation of these continuing for fifteen years. For their part, the trades union in the building industry agreed to reduce their apprenticeship requirements so that the labour force could be expanded quickly. Meanwhile private funds flowed rapidly into the burgeoning building society movement, seeking a safe haven from the vagaries of the inter-war Stock Exchange (Boddy, 1980 p.13). House building was also helped by the rising real incomes of those who were in work during the inter-war period and by falling building costs for materials between 1924 and 1933 (Heady, 1978 p.131).

2.3   THE POST-WAR PERIOD

However there was still a long way to go by the end of the Second World War. The rate of building for ownership had been truly imp-ressive, though less progress had been made for the low-income groups, particularly after 1933 when general subsidies on council house construction for general need were removed. Inter-war local authority housing was mostly for the better-off employees in regular work, since there were no rent rebates and there was a flat rate of subsidy for new houses. As standards rose, more rural houses could be classified as unfit - perhaps 20 per cent by 1945. Also 208,000 houses had been destroyed in the Second World War, another half million made unin-habitable and many more had deteriorated due to six years' lack of maintenance (Heady, 1978 p.136). Although most of the damage was in the cities, rural housing inevitably took second place to restoring the cities in the immediate post-war years. In 1942 the Scott Report on Land Utilisation in Rural Areas was still able to make disparaging comments on rural housing as well as bring new policy issues into prominence.

'Conditions under which rural workers had to live were another contributory reason for the drift (to the towns). Housing, in particular, was a serious problem, rural cottages generally being far below the modern standards of housing for the working classes. In spite of the falling numbers of the rural population, there was a growing shortage of housing accommodation in many districts, largely due to cottages being rented by other than farm workers. Over the country, generally, many rural workers were living in cottages which should have been condemned as uninhabitable.

The wages of agricultural workers were too low for them to pay an economic rent for the right kind of house and in consequence the building of cottages offered no attraction to the speculative builder. Such housing accommodation as had been built specially for agricultural workers had been erected almost entirely by the landowners, including farmers owning their own farms. As a result many workers were living in 'tied' cottages or in cottages which, although not 'tied' to a farm, belonged to a local estate owner and were held by the worker on an understood condition that he was employed on work connected with the estate.

The worker in a 'tied' cottage is liable to be evicted at any time he has a dispute with his employer or when, for any reason, the employer decides to replace him by another worker. He does not enjoy protection under the Rent Restrictions Acts as he can be evicted without any alternative accommodation being provided for him. If he loses his job he also loses his home.

(...) where cottages are not tied to the farm there is a real danger that they may be acquired by town-dwellers for week-ends or holidays. There is no doubt that one contributory cause of the housing shortage for rural workers has lain in the growth of the 'week-end' habit. Indeed, many city workers lived permanently in country cottages travelling to and from their work daily. Their houses were often agricultural cottages bought because of their picturesque character and brought up-to-date with all modern conveniences.

Apart from actual shortage of cottages, the general standard of accommodation, equipment and services was - and still is - very low. Thousands of cottages have no piped water supply, no gas or electric light, no third bedroom and often only one living room with no separate cooking and scullery accommodation. For the great majority of rural workers a bathroom is a rare luxury. In many cases too, the modern country cottages seem to have been planned from an urban standpoint with little or no regard to the special requirements of the country worker. There is often no shed or room for taking off and drying wet clothes; no storage room for stocks of foodstuffs, seeds, etc.; no sheds for garden tools or bicycles. Such conditions undoubtedly drove many of the better type of young rural workers into other occupations. Many a young farm worker wanting to get married has found it impossible to rent a cottage at all, or else if he obtained one, his pros-

pective bride found it difficult to reconcile herself to living
in a cottage with inadequate accommodation and no amenities.
As the result they either deserted the country for the town, or
according to the evidence of the Federation of Women's Institutes,
restricted the size of their family to only one child.'
                (Ministry of Works and Planning, 1942 pp. 17-18).

This lengthy extract from the Scott Report shows how the report,
like Janus, looks back to the old and forward to the new. It con-
tains old concerns and new preoccupations. There are echoes here of
the Victorian concern for the poor structural quality of the houses
and overcrowding. Even in 1952, 29 per cent of rural houses were in
need of major repairs and 12 per cent were beyond repair and unfit
for habitation. As recently as 1936 the Ministry of Health had
published a report on overcrowding though now the concern was less
over morality and more with health and privacy. The Scott Report
showed that housing policy was still set firmly in the context of
reducing rural migration - a migration which had progressed so far
that it was called depopulation. Poor housing was viewed as a
stimulus to migration but this was now feared more for its effect on
those left behind in the countryside - fewer services and a smaller
farm labour force - than for its effect in exacerbating urban
problems. There is clear evidence that the inter-war concern for
minimum standards of housing had been accepted as not merely as a
desirable target but an entitlement which government ought to aid
people to acquire. The report noted the low pay of rural workers
which in relative terms was as true then as it was seventy years
earlier. An average farm worker's wage in 1939 was between 32s. and
37s. 6d. for a 50 to 54 hour working week while even unskilled
industrial labourers - if they had a job - were earning 43s. to 60s.
for a 42 to 48 hour week. This made the unsubsidised upgrading of
farm labourer's accommodation a very slow process. The Scott Report
noted with disapproval the low standard of service provision in rural
areas - services which would have been beyond all reasonable
expectation in the countryside fifty years before. One-third of
rural dwellings had no electricity supply in 1939 and probably only
eight per cent of farms had mains electricity - a few more had their
own generators. Over a million people in the countryside had no
piped water supply and 46 per cent of parishes had no system of
sewerage (Ministry of Works and Planning, 1942 p.69).

However, the Report also expressed new concerns which were developing and which in time would become the principal issues of public
policy in this field. There was anxiety over the effect of isolation
on the health and education of rural families - clearly an indication
of how far depopulation had progressed. There were doubts over the
cost of providing services unimagined fifty years earlier to every
house in the countryside, however isolated it might be. These doubts
would lead in time to proposals, which will be examined in the next
chapter, for the spatial concentration of country people so as to
cheapen the provision of services. The Report also highlighted the
question of the tied cottage. The Labour Party was already committed
to abolishing them although the Report could not agree to this. There

was also some disapproval of the purchase of country properties by large numbers of 'week-enders' - they would now be called second-home owners - and urban commuters.

The Scott Report was not just a mirror of past and future issues. It was a document with its own standpoint and it was influential. The Report was much concerned to promote what in 1942 was a long forgotten sight - a stable and prosperous agriculture. The Report believed that this by itself would revive rural areas more than anything else. Indeed other policies should be so framed that they would aid the prosperity of farming. To this end industry should be kept away from the open country whenever possible and should be directed to the towns. Industry in the countryside was seen as undesirable on six grounds and the only exceptions the Scott Committee envisaged were for industry clearly connected with farming or forestry which used female or juvenile labour.

'Arguments against industry in the countryside

(i)   Loss of productive agricultural land.

(ii) Dislocation of farming and break-up of farm units.

(iii) Harmful effects on agricultural production by noxious fumes and poisonous effluents.

(iv) Attraction of labour, especially the younger workers, away from agriculture.

(v)   Social disturbance through contact between rural and urban mentalities.

(vi) Spoliation of the beauty of the countryside by bad siting and bad design of buildings.

These effects resulted mainly from the congregation of industry on the outskirts of big cities. They are obviously likely to be magnified if industry is dispersed into the heart of country areas, and particularly if it were sited in villages or in the open countryside.

We have carefully considered the advantages which it is claimed the introduction of these industrial units into villages or the open countryside would bring. We believe that the maintenance of agriculture, together with the steps recommended in Chapter VII, will in themselves have the effect of reviving country life and bringing about an improvement in the physical and social standards of country areas.

The provision of alternative occupations for women and young people would be of advantage but certain dangers might be involved, as for instance, the attraction away from agriculture of the younger generation and the causing of discontent, at least amongst their menfolk, by attracting married women from their households for full-time paid employment. If industrial units were sited in existing or new small towns in country areas, they would rely less on labour from purely agricultural communities, and for those in the villages who so desired it would be possible to take up employment in the nearby town factories without living away from home.

Summarizing, we recommend that industry should be encouraged first to make use of vacant or derelict sites in towns and that where industries are brought into country areas they should be located in existing or new small towns and not in villages or the open country.

On balance we consider the introduction of carefully regulated industry in this way would be beneficial to the countryside'
                    (Ministry of Works and Planning, 1942 p.69).

Additional house building in rural areas was seen as an urgent requirement, even if more expensive than urban construction and there was a new concern in the Report for design and layout. Rural houses, it was felt, should look rural and be in harmony with their region and should not be suburban designs transported to the countryside. Although this aesthetic concern was new to government reports there had been private individuals much exercised by the need for rural buildings to be in keeping with the locality (Wordsworth, 1835 pp.72-81). Rural houses should be built so as to minimise the loss of farmland, and especially good quality farmland, and be a part of villages rather than spread out in open country. There was a concern to protect agriculture from competition for both employment and land while at the same time preserving the visual character of the English and Welsh countryside. Partly this was to be achieved by keeping out large-scale industry and through the control of building materials but also it would be achieved through the prosperity of farming - farmers being seen as the guardians and gardeners of the countryside. It was assumed that farmers would pass on their new-found prosperity in due proportion as higher farm wages and improvements to tied houses. In a trenchant Minority Report, Dennison objected to the privileged status being accorded to farming in peace-time by the Scott Committee and he pointed to the opportunity cost of the resources of land, labour and capital devoted to farming. He argued that in many cases they would be used more productively in another industry. In short, if farm workers wages are so much lower than those of industrial workers then let farm workers move to industrial jobs to the benefit of themselves and the national economy. The economic weight of this argument failed to convince the Committee, however, and the development of the British planning system since 1947 has followed the Scott Report's recommendations rather than Dennison's.

Agriculture has been protected from the high rate of loss of land in the 1930s by higher urban densities, by production subsidies and by its favoured position in public inquiries into specific developments and district development plans. The National Parks, Green Belts and

similar devices have further sought to maintain landscape character
while building in open countryside has normally been prohibited
except in the special case of agricultural and similar workers who
have to live on the farm.

2.4 CURRENT ISSUES

Since the middle of last century the nature of the rural housing
problem has changed. Even by the standards of the last quarter of the
twentieth century, overcrowding is no longer a widespread problem in
rural Britain. Concern over the moral welfare of the rural population
is rarely expressed within the context of housing policy while the net
drift to the cities has slowed to such a trickle that it is no longer
of any significance in terms of urban development. The physical
standard of rural houses has improved steadily and the housing stock
is now much younger than ever before. The Scott Report was undoubtedly correct in forecasting that a more prosperous agriculture
would improve housing to some extent and this can also be said of the
more general increase in living standards throughout the countryside.
People have more money to improve houses, they can afford better
houses and government can spend more building new houses and giving
grants to improve existing ones. In 1971 the House Improvement Survey
showed a remarkably large decline of 41 per cent in the number of
unfit rural houses in England and Wales since 1967 (Rogers, 1976 p.
102).

The progress towards better houses has been marked but uneven and
concentrations of poorer housing are still found in north-east
Scotland, Wales, East Anglia, Cornwall and the Peak District (Census
Research Unit, 1980 pp.72-3). In Scotland there is still a disparity
between urban and rural housing as Table 1 shows for 1971. Although
the allocation of regions to the urban and rural categories is
necessarily crude, the rural areas appear to have the poorer housing,
though not markedly so, by two of the three criteria. It may be
anticipated that the 1981 census will show further improvement in
both areas. In England and Wales, the House Condition Survey of 1971
showed that, in contrast to Scotland, rural housing was generally
better than urban housing (Rogers, 1976 p.103), although the House
Condition Survey of 1976 came to the opposite conclusion on the basis
of a sample survey of 215 local authorities (Dunn, Rawson and Rogers,
1981 p.43).

The moderate spatial disparity in rural housing standards is paral-
leled by a rather greater disparity in the standard of housing of
different socio-economic groups. Workers in the lower-paid occupations
such as catering, retailing and farming remain unable to afford the
better type of housing unless other members of their families also
have paid employment. This may mean that a concern with absolute
standards of housing has been replaced by consideration of the relative
standards of housing. Yet there remain groups of people who still
have an unacceptably low standard of housing. They have to live
without basic amenities, are homeless or they have to live with parents
or in a caravan. Whereas formerly they could look to the private

TABLE 1. Urban and rural housing conditions in Scotland, 1971

Percentage of houses lacking one or more of the three basic amenities

Urban regions	13.1
Rural regions	15.4

Percentage of houses below tolerable standard

Urban regions	11.5
Rural regions	17.9

Percentage of households living at over $1\frac{1}{2}$ persons per room

Urban regions	7.1
Rural regions	3.7

rented sector for housing they could afford, cheap houses for rent have become increasingly scarce as rising property prices and control of rents have encouraged the owners of rented property to sell their houses. Ironically the legislation which provided short-term relief to the lower paid by controlling rents has had the long-term effect of worsening their housing situation. The houses themselves may well be in a much better state of repair with all the basic amenities now installed but the improvement in the quality of the housing stock does not guarantee the improvement in the housing conditions of those formerly poorly housed.

The great strides made in the provision of council houses have not yet solved totally the problem of housing the lowest paid for a number of reasons. The focus of attention for local authorities and centrally -funded house-building organisations has been urban rather than rural. The slums of the cities were so numerous, so visible and so widely condemned that the country areas, being less obviously needy, received less finance than they might have wished and little recognition of the greater costs involved in council-house building in the remoter areas. After the mid-1960s the rate of publicly-financed house building in Britain declined by forty per cent by 1973 and by much more in Scotland and Wales and the trend has intensified since 1977 (Rogers, 1976 p.99). The amount of private building has fluctuated from year to year but on average has been reduced by less. In rural areas the proportion of council houses remains low at about twenty-two per cent in rural England and twenty-seven per cent in rural Wales compared with twenty-nine per cent in England and Wales as a whole. In Scotland it is over fifty per cent which is again lower than the figure for the whole country of fifty-five per cent. In some regions the proportion of council housing is even lower than these figures indicate, particu-

larly in north Wales, Lancashire and south and south-west England
(Census Research Unit, 1980 pp.68-9). In addition the provision of
council housing has had to swim against the tide of the growth in
many rural areas of essentially urban house-buyers who compete directly
or indirectly for housing with local people. The essence of housing
policy should still focus on the lower paid although the context of
their housing has changed radically during the last 150 years.

Nothing exemplifies this change more clearly than the growth in
legislation over aesthetic and land-use considerations. Where houses
are built, how they are built and what they look like are now major
issues not only in the National Parks but also in most other parts of
the countryside to a lesser but still substantial degree. The
countryside has changed enormously since last century, not so much
in its visual appearance as in who lives there and how they earn
their living. The countryside has become a kind of national property
since it is now accessible to so many and large numbers of townspeople live there.

The next chapter will examine how the protagonists and the forms of
argument involved in housing policy have changed, so that the context
of rural planning generally and planning for housing in particular
has been transformed since 1945. In Chapter 4 a detailed case study
will be presented of how these protagonists and attitudes to the
countryside have influenced housing and planning in the Lake District
National Park.

3. Current Issues in Housing and Planning

Rus in urbe.   Martial (b. A.D. 43) Epigrammata

Urbs in rure.   R.E. Pahl (1965)

The aspects of rural housing which have excited most political and popular interest have changed during the last century. Two of the issues which have aroused much debate in the 1970s have been tied cottages and key settlement policy. These have concerned, respectively, the terms on which agricultural employees are provided with houses by farmers and the rationale for allocating houses and services between the many hamlets and villages in the countryside. It is useful to examine these issues, since they form part of the national background to the case-study in the next chapter of the relationship between housing policy and rural planning in the Lake District. They also serve to demonstrate the attitudes and priorities at work in the countryside since the end of the Second World War.

3.1 TIED COTTAGES

The term 'tied cottage' has come to be synonymous with the countryside but in practice people in many walks of life find themselves living in accommodation owned by their employer. The Prime Minister, university vice-chancellors, miners, nurses, vicars, soldiers and policemen may all live in tied accommodation. Concern over the effects of having a single person as employer and landlord originated last century. The 'closed villages' of England, where one person owned all the land and houses, were identified early in the nineteenth century as a contributory factor in rural migration where this power was abused. If the landowner developed a grudge against an employee or tenant, then he could lose both house and job. There was created a society where outward conformity and deference were necessary to retain one's landlord's goodwill. Such closed villages are rarer today although two, Great Barrington and Great Tew (Oxfordshire) have attained notoriety since the landlords have allowed houses to stand empty rather than re-let them to 'outsiders'. On a larger scale, the lack of choice in housing engendered by this monopoly could mean wholesale migration to other villages and towns as the poor law after 1795 encouraged landowners to limit the supply of housing to those with jobs. Some landowners pulled down houses which might be occupied by people who would be a charge on those who were wealthy enough to contribute to the poor-law funds. Even when this practice became less necessary with the formation of poor-law unions between parishes in 1834, the precariousness of the worker's position was still evident. In the decades between 1870 and the First World War, the tied cottage was frequently discussed for its possible effects in promoting rural depopulation, the scale of which was then of great concern. It was argued that it was less the actual evictions which drove a few people to the cities as the fear of eviction which haunted the majority. The loss of self-respect caused by depending on one person for house and income was believed to lead to urban migration for peace of mind as much as for a more secure job or a higher wage. Thompson (1945 p.6) noted in Oxfordshire in the 1880s how important a free choice of house was for the villagers.

'Some labourers in other villages worked on farms or estates where they had their cottages rent free; but the hamlet people did not envy them, for "Stands to reason," they said, "they've allus got to do just what they be told, or out they goes, neck and crop, bag and baggage." A shilling, or even two shillings a week, they felt, was not too much to pay for the freedom to live and vote as they liked and to go to church or chapel or neither as they preferred.'

It was probably this lack of freedom which led the Labour Party advocate the abolition of the system - a pledge they made in nearly every election manifesto after 1945. However it was not until 1976 that legislation was introduced to amend a system which had survived well over a century of criticism. This remarkable resilience needs to be examined carefully since it reveals much about attitudes and power in rural policy.

The causes of the disquiet about agricultural tied cottages are quite evident. Whereas nineteenth-century industrialists who built houses for their workers usually sold them within a number of years, farmers tended to build more tied cottages as the century progressed, particularly in Scotland and northern England where communal housing for workers (bothies) and the tradition of workers living in the farmers' houses were dying out. Similarly, just as some industrialists built tied houses of superior quality, Port Sunlight for example, so there were a few farmers and estates which did the same. The agricultural workers' position was worsened because, unlike miners who also had poor quality houses, their industry was not nationalised. After 1947 the National Coal Board had the resources to improve miners' rows and the political power to persuade local authorities - often Labour controlled - to build sufficient new council houses for miners. The farming industry did not have access to central government funds, being a dispersed and fragmented industry of several hundred thousand farmers. Newby (1978 pp.65-71) has argued that those areas where the landed interest controlled local government were often the ones with many tied cottages and where local expenditure on houses, among other things, was minimised.

Prior to 1976, the legal position of the occupier of an agricultural tied cottage was much less clear-cut than the polarised debate suggested. Gasson identified three types of relationship between the farmer who owned the house and his employee who occupied it. The employee might be either a service tenant, a service licensee or an ordinary licensee (Gasson, 1975 pp.92-6). The service tenant was permitted to occupy his employer's house and was in a similar legal position to any other tenant of a house. He·enjoyed the security of tenure provided under the Rent Acts, this protection being considerable except between 1957 and 1965. However, even service tenants could lose their house when their employment by the landlord ceased since the County Court might grant the farmer a repossession order. This was only granted when the farmer could demonstrate that his former employee's accommodation was reasonably required for another person with whom the farmer already had a contract of employment. These were broader and rather more likely conditions for repossession than for non-agricultural workers with a service tenancy.

The farm workers who were service licensees were in a weaker position since they had no tenancy agreement with the farmer separate from their contract of employment. This group comprised those who were required, rather than simply permitted to occupy a specific house for the better performance of their duties. A stockman might be required to live in a particular house because he had to be near the animals night and day to look after them properly. Such a person had to leave the house when his employment ceased and, although the farmer could not evict him, a repossession order had to be granted to the farmer in all cases.

The only redress the service tenants and licensees eventually acquired was contained in the Rent (Agriculture) Act 1965 (s 33) and the Agriculture Act 1970 (s 99) which allowed the courts to suspend the repossession order until six months or, in some cases, twelve months after the worker's employment ended. Prior to 1965 only one month's grace was given. This extended period allowed time for the worker to find other accommodation but even this respite was not mandatory. The court could choose not to suspend the repossession order in cases where it believed suspension would harm the farmer more than the worker, or where the running of the farm would suffer, or where damage was occurring to the property, or where alternative accommodation was or soon would be available for the worker.

The final group, ordinary licensees, had the least protection since they were in the same position as lodgers in a private house. They had no tenancy agreement and the owner could require them to leave his house at any time without having to justify this in court.

The difficulty for the agricultural worker was partly one of not knowing which category he was in. Consequently, there were no national figures on tenancies and licences and so he did not know his rights. Whichever category he was in, he could find himself jobless and homeless in quick succession unlike most other tenants. Since rural areas usually have fewer council houses than the cities and house purchase was normally beyond the means of low-paid farm workers, the potential for distress was considerable.

It was a potential which faced a great many farm workers. Gasson (1975 p.35) estimated that 58.7 per cent of the full-time hired workers covered by the Farm Management Survey of 1972-3 lived in tied accommodation - a figure which agrees closely with an independent estimate from the Wages and Employment Enquiry of 1972. This represented about 100,000 to 112,000 tied cottages in Great Britain - a figure which had been falling but less rapidly than the decline in the size of the farm labour force. Consequently the proportion of farm workers in tied accommodation had risen although there were considerable regional variations around the national average. In Dumfriesshire 98 per cent of full-time hired workers lived in tied accommodation which reflected its above average prevalence throughout central and southern Scotland (Figure 4). Tied cottages were much less prevalent in Wales (about 30 cottages per 100 full-time hired workers) and Lancashire/Yorkshire (about 37 cottages per 100 full-time hired workers). Gasson has suggested that differences in the practices for hiring workers last century may help explain this variation but the mechanism is not clear and this topic deserves much more research. The incidence of tied cottages was greatest for specialist livestock workers and lowest for general workers, those in horticulture and for new types of farming like large-scale poultry production (Table 2). Tied cottages were also relatively uncommon on small farms with only one or two employees.

Although the origins of the tied cottage system are far from recent, the evidence suggests that the last forty years has seen the system assume increasing importance. Between 1945 and the early 1970s the proportion of farm workers in tied cottages increased by around 20 percentage points. There is some debate over how this should be interpreted. It could indicate that, as the farm labour force has declined, those in tied cottages have been trapped in farming by the housing. Alternatively, it could be that as urban demand for houses in the countryside has increased, more potential employees are insisting on a house with the job, particularly the more skilled livestock workers who are in shortest supply. This could explain the reversal in the distribution of tied cottages in England since a study in 1932 by the Inter-Departmental Committee on Agricultural Tied Cottages. This reported that they were more prevalent in northern rather than southern England although Figure 4 shows that, by and large, the reverse was true in 1972-73. A greater degree of urban intrusion into the countryside in the south could be used to explain this. In short, the last forty years has seen the tied cottage assume greater importance in the housing of agricultural workers in Great Britain. The debate on the merits of the system is therefore one of growing relevance in the 1970s.

In 1942 the Scott Report rehearsed the arguments which then applied to tied cottages.

"... Over the country generally, many rural workers were living in cottages which should have been condemned as uninhabitable.

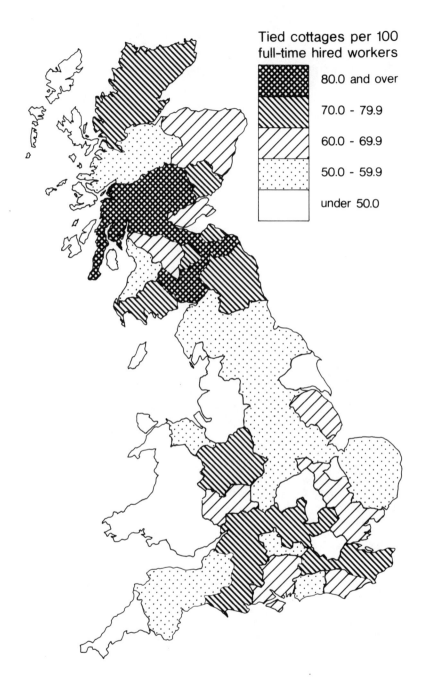

Tied cottages per 100
full-time hired workers

80.0 and over

70.0 - 79.9

60.0 - 69.9

50.0 - 59.9

under 50.0

FIG.4.   Tied cottages in Great Britain, 1972-3 (after Gasson, 1975).

TABLE 2. Cottage provision by occupation of worker, 1971-3

Type of Occupation	Cottages per 100 full-time hired men, 1971-73 mean
Dairy cowman	80.1
Foreman, bailiff	70.3
Other stockman	61.5
Tractor driver	60.1
General farm worker	46.9
Other farm worker	37.1
Market garden worker	18.6
All full-time hired men	52.9

Source: Wages and Employment Enquiry quoted in Gasson (1975) p.17.

The wages of agricultural workers were too low for them to pay an economic rent for the right kind of house and in consequence the building of cottages offered no attraction to the speculative builder. (...) As a result many workers were living in 'tied' cottages or in cottages which, although not 'tied' to a farm, belonged to a local estate owner and were held by the worker on an understood condition that he was employed on work connected with the estate.

The worker in a 'tied' cottage is liable to be evicted at any time he has a dispute with his employer or when, for any reason, the employer decides to replace him by another worker. He does not enjoy protection under the Rent Restrictions Acts as he can be evicted without any alternative accommodation being provided for him. If he loses his job he also loses his home.

Another great disadvantage of the 'tied' cottage is that, being on or near farm premises, the worker and his family are often isolated from village life. This is a particular hardship on women - and more especially on younger women - who in the majority of cases find such an existence lonely and inconvenient because of the distance from a shopping centre or from a school for the children. As a result, the health of the women and children as well as the education of the family, which should be paramount, may suffer. There is also the added difficulty of providing isolated cottages with modern conveniences such as electricity, water supply, or a nearby telephone.

On the other hand from the farmer's point of view there is
a great advantage in the workers - particularly those in charge
of livestock - living on the spot. They contend that the
health and care of the animals would suffer gravely if the
horseman or cowman were not readily available by night as well
as by day should necessity arise. Moreover with the long
hours that must often be worked in agriculture, it is a great
saving whether of working time or of their own brief leisure
time if workers live close at hand. In addition, while
housing in rural areas remains scarce great difficulties
may be caused by cottages not being tied to the job. Workers
may leave the land and yet continue to live in their cottages
with the result that accommodation is not available for the
agricultural workers essential for the working of surrounding
farms.

Moreover where cottages are not tied to the farm there is
a real danger that they may be acquired by town-dwellers for
week-ends or holidays. There is no doubt that one contributory cause of the housing shortage for rural workers has
lain in the growth of the 'week-end' habit. Indeed, many
city workers lived permanently in country cottages travelling
to and from their work daily. Their houses were often
agricultural cottages bought because of their picturesque
character and brought up-to-date with all modern conveniences."
                Ministry of Planning and Works (1942) paras.56-61.

Although the period of which the Scott Committee were writing in
1942 was different from today in many ways and the dominance of tied
accommodation in farm workers' housing much less marked, nonetheless
the basic conflict was the same. In the system's favour it could be
said that workers were available near the farm which might be
essential or at least convenient depending on the type of farming.
Through his houses the farmer had an inducement to attract good
skilled workers and most farmers and the National Farmers Union
supported the system strongly for this reason. Fletcher (1975 p.
174) found in a survey in Devon that 92 per cent of farmers believed
their workers (though perhaps not other farmers' workers) were happy
with the arrangement. The farmer could afford to pay lower wages
because of the lower rent he charged for the cottage. For the farm
workers, accommodation was available much more cheaply than in the
private rented sector, often with a garden and low travel costs to
work. Because of the increase in urban pressure on the countryside,
alternative low-cost housing for renting was not plentiful. Against
the system, it could be argued that it promoted the maintenance of
low wages and occupational immobility since even the possibility of
the loss of one's home could produce an unhealthy servility into the
relationship between employer and employee. In addition the corollary
of proximity to the farm was often isolation from schools, shops and
other services. The housing position of a worker retiring from a
low-pay industry with few savings could be acute if he was not allowed
to stay on in the house.

The survey by Fletcher in the Tiverton district of Devon threw some light on how the system was viewed by farmer and worker. The main difference seemed to be between the younger and older workers. For the former, the very low rents and good condition of their houses were very positive factors in favour of the tied cottage. Although the older workers also paid low rents, their houses were in much poorer condition, older, with fewer facilities and much less recent modernisation. Only 37 per cent of farm cottages in Great Britain were built after 1918 compared with 65 per cent of the country's total housing stock (Gasson, 1975 p.64). The age of the cottages became even more noticeable in the areas most distant from large towns where the attraction of industrial jobs was less. The implication is that farmers were not modernising the older workers' houses because there was little chance they could get another job whereas this was a real possibility with younger workers. Fletcher found that there had been much less movement between jobs among the older workers in the five years preceding his survey.

The farm workers themselves were divided about the system. Few wished to concede anything in its favour even when one-third of them paid no rent at all for their house. The disadvantages of the system in terms of insecurity were frequently mentioned even though only 4 per cent of the interviewees had even been evicted or threatened with this. Many worried about the difficulty the tied cottage system created when they wanted to leave farming or move to a better paid farming job. Nearly forty per cent of the sample of workers wanted to leave agriculture and nine-tenths felt that their tied accommodation hindered this although for only one in ten were problems with accommodation a direct reason for wishing to leave farming.

The unfavourable attitudes to tied cottages among workers were not militant but were probably widespread, although some regional variation in attitudes was evident in the contrasting stances of the main English and Welsh trade union for farm workers, the National Union of Agricultural and Allied Workers (N.U.A.A.W.) and the Scottish workers' union, which is a section of the very large and powerful Transport and General Workers Union. Whereas the English and Welsh union was strongly opposed to the tied cottage system, the Scottish union did not press strongly for its abolition, despite its greater importance in Scotland. This may be because evictions in Scotland were extremely rare. Court cases in England for repossession were certainly not numerous, estimates range from 1,000 to 1,200 a year with perhaps 200 to 300 evictions (Rogers, 1976 p.108). Newby gives lower estimates of about 560 court cases in 1973 and about 20 evictions a year (Newby, 1977 p.180). This may have been sufficient to keep the issue alive particularly in the arable areas of eastern England where union support has traditionally been highest. Certainly some evictions were a mutually agreed ploy between farmer and worker to ensure that, as a homeless person, the worker would go to the top of the council's waiting list for a house. In some areas however the council defined losing one's farm job as intentional homelessness which, until the late 1970s, was grounds for absolving the council from the obligation to rehouse. Much depended on how well the worker and farmer got on together and on how the local authority interpreted its duties.

It is not clear why the Labour Party failed to legislate to alter the tied cottage system when they were in government between 1945 and 1951 and between 1964 and 1970. Perhaps they were preoccupied with housing and social welfare in the urban and industrial areas from which they derived so much of their support. The lack of action may also be a tribute to the persuasiveness of the agricultural lobby at Westminster and Whitehall. By the mid-1970s however a leading official of the N.U.A.A.W., Miss Joan Maynard, had also achieved a leading post on the Executive of the Labour Party and this may have helped the reform group. The legislation which was passed in 1976, the Rent (Agriculture) Act, converted all English and Welsh agricultural tenancies into statutory tenancies protected by the Rent Acts. The only exceptions were where the landlord was the Crown (the Crown Estate Commissioners opposed the measure) or the Duchies of Cornwall or Lancaster (The Times, 6 January 1976).

Under the terms of the 1976 Act, the landlord could still request the court to grant him a possession order for the house but this would only be granted where there was suitable alternative accommodation for the worker or where the worker was a statutory nuisance, had failed to pay rent or maintain the house, or had unreasonably refused other suitable accommodation. The landlord could also regain possession of the house if he had contracted to sell or let the house to another worker and would be seriously prejudiced if he could not regain the house. Similarly if the farmer wanted the house for himself, his family or his parents he would always be able to regain it.

The local authority meanwhile had the following duty imposed on it.

"If the local authority are satisfied that the applicant's (ie the farmer's) case is substantiated (...) they shall use their best endeavours to provide the suitable accommodation, and in assessing under this subsection the priority to be given to meet the applicant's case, the authority shall take into account the urgency of the case, the competing claims on the accommodation which they can provide and the resources at their disposal."

Rent (Agriculture) Act 1976, S 28 (7).

Clearly the system outlined here is a compromise. The General Secretary of the N.U.A.A.W., Mr. Reg Bottini, described it as removing the fear of homelessness by which he conceded that tied accommodation had not been abolished as his union had sought since 1894 (The Times, 5 May 1976 and 17 May 1976). The National Farmers Union (N.F.U.) described it as far from what farmers had feared. Despite the existence of a Labour Government which could have used the guillotine procedure in the House of Commons to enact a more radical measure, the farmers had managed to secure the principle that they

needed houses on farms for current workers. The involvement of the
local authority was a device to secure the removal of workers from
tied houses without the political embarrassment and personal hardship
of repossession or homelessness. The Conservative and Liberal peers
in the House of Lords tried to make the local authorities' duty to
rehouse mandatory in all cases and put a limit of three months on the
process but these amendments were removed by the Commons and virtually
the original Bill became law at the end of 1976. The Act represented
a compromise between, on the one hand, the abolition of tied cottages
and, on the other, the farmers' case that removing their freedom to
repossess houses from former workers would jeopardise farm production.
However, the compromise was not achieved in Parliament where few
opposition amendments to the original Bill were approved. Rather it
was achieved before the Bill arrived at Westminster and here the
strength of the National Farmers Union was vital. Not only was
abolition avoided but local authorities were given an extra housing
burden without any compensating action to raise the supply of houses
in the countryside. The tied houses in farming represent about ten
per cent of the tied accommodation in Britain but no other group
obtained the special, though not absolute, priority for council
housing accorded to farm workers. It was a compromise which could
not have been proposed in earlier years when farm workers were still
leaving the industry in large numbers.

Initially the system worked well. Farmers could submit a case to
the local Agricultural Dwelling Housing Advisory Committee that it
was essential that a farm worker be rehoused and, if the Committee
agreed that there was no alternative accommodation, the local
authority would have to rehouse him. Burke (1981 p.101) recorded
that some authorities were unwilling to accept the duty and there
remained the fact that the supply of council houses in rural areas
is limited. Larkin (1978) noted that some authorities would only
give their poorest housing to former agricultural workers. There is
clearly scope for more research into the functioning of these three-
man committees.

The issue of tied houses is an interesting one because it was one
of the few foci of concerted discontent in the usually amicable
relationship between farmer and worker. It was also a difficult
issue to resolve since repossession was so drastic a step and the two
sides were hardly talking the same language.

The farmers' case was argued on pragmatic grounds of low rents, house
supply, animal welfare and efficient husbandry. These were all fair
points and so the preferred solution on the farmers' side was to
control the few rogue farmers who abused the system and caused unnecessary hardship. Early warning systems were suggested and
charters of good conduct such as the Warnford Charter were proposed.
Some union officials also saw fair play as the solution.

"Everybody understands that a farmer must have a cottage
back after a man has left his employment but much more
common-sense and sympathy is needed during the change-over

It should never come to an eviction"

(Blythe, 1972 p.108).

The worker's case was argued on principle. The system, they argued, was wrong in itself being demeaning and eroded independence and choice of employment. In public neither side could argue the case on the other's terms. Real dialogue was impossible. A resolution was highly unlikely without the government as arbiter to bring the sides together and solve this agricultural problem by making the housing prospects for rural non-farm workers worse than they would otherwise have been. More direct solutions such as building more council houses were financially impossible for the government while paying workers sufficient so they could afford not to live in a low-rent tied cottage and could make a career in farming was financially impossible for some farmers. Whilst there are farmers who pay sufficiently over the statutory minimum farm wage to allow this, others, where profits are low or the competition for labour from non-agricultural employers is weak, are unable or unwilling to follow suit.

The Rent (Agriculture) Act 1976 was a classic British compromise which pleased few, was just acceptable to the majority and was practicable because it failed to meet the fundamental objectives of, and objections from, each side. Ten years earlier, even this compromise would scarcely have been practicable since the extra burden of rehousing it would have placed on local authorities would have been too great. Clearly, delay allowed an impasse to be resolved by a compromise. On these grounds the policy on tied cottages can be said to be an unexceptional part of British rural planning.

3.2 KEY SETTLEMENT POLICY

The second area of debate recently at the interface of housing and planning has concerned the size of rural settlements and the study of this topic reveals some other common traits of rural planning. The starting point was an unwillingness by local authorities, and not only those in Great Britain, to allow new housing and other facilities to be placed anywhere in the countryside that private interests wished. This frequently expressed itself as a desire to move population up the urban hierarchy so that fewer people would live in the smallest settlements. In the United Kingdom this was called key settlement policy and Cloke judged it to have been 'the principal agent of planned change in post-war rural Britain' (Cloke, 1979 p.vii).

Any desire for a spatial concentration of the rural population in nineteenth-century Britain would have been almost impossible to implement since local and national government had such limited powers. Nevertheless there was a feeling then that larger rural settlements had the potential to slow down the drift of people to the cities. The cities needed to be protected from too many new inhabitants since conditions were so poor for many of the existing townsfolk, while the countryside could ill afford the social consequences of depopulation, the loss of a farm labour force and a smaller reserve of sturdy, healthy recruits for the armed forces. The larger villages had the potential

to raise the social and cultural standards of the countryside. In so
far as urban migration was a move to secure better wages and personal
freedom, the physical improvement of the village was scarcely relevant.
However it did have a deeper value in so far as it could raise the
intellectual and moral standards of the rural population as well as
the purely material conditions of life. It was this and the associated
notions of rural self-sufficiency and self-improvement mentally and
economically which appealed to Harold Peake (1922) and Henry Morris.
While Morris was Chief Education Officer for Cambridgeshire between
1922 and 1954, he used village colleges as the vehicle for this
general uplifting of the rural community (Rée, 1973). This focal point
for general and agricultural schooling, social functions and, above all,
adult education was designed to so raise standards that the village
could develop an appeal which would counter the siren call of the city.
It would also promote better parish administration (Morris, 1925).
The idea was taken up by Morris's colleagues and pupils in Somerset,
Leicestershire and Cumberland but principle and practice had to be
reconciled over money. Only ten village colleges were planned by
Morris for Cambridgeshire so the cost of developing them effectively
created two classes of settlement - some had colleges and most did
not. Although this was intended to be temporary, it was in fact
permanent.

The second tangle of ideas leading up to key settlement policy can
be seen in the Scott Report of 1942. This started by noting and
deploring the 'drift from the land'.

"The drift was greatest among the younger generation of
farm workers for whom there remained few opportunities in
the country and to whom the attractions of industry and of
town life appealed most, a fact which is shown very vividly by
the fall in the numbers of young male workers under 21 - a
fall of some 75,000 or nearly 44 per cent between 1921-24
and 1938, as compared with a fall of 103,000 or 19 per cent
in the number of male workers over 21 during the same period.
The love of the country and country life is an innate
national characteristic and in a large number of cases the
'pull' of the towns is economic. The countryside suffered
from a grave inferiority of wages and opportunities for
advancement and from inadequate housing and services.

The depressed condition of agriculture inevitably had
repercussions on other rural occupations, with the result
that migration of labour was not confined to workers on
the land. Thus village craftsmen such as blacksmiths,
saddlers, carpenters and wheelwrights also felt the wave
of depression. (...)

Even many of those employed in the ancillary occupations
of rural life - assistants in village shops, rural road
workers and railwaymen - wherever possible 'bettered'
themselves by getting a job in the town. Even in the County
Constabulary a move to a town was looked upon as 'promotion'.

Wives and daughters also followed the example of, or set the
example to, their menfolk by going into factories. The
result was a growing depopulation of the countryside and a
set back to country life."
                    (Ministry of Planning and Works, 1942 paras. 52-3).

The policy to reverse this situation followed logically. It was to
improve 'housing and general living conditions and so (equalize)
economic, social and educational opportunities in town and country that
those who prefer country life will no longer find themselves and their
children at a permanent disadvantage' (para. 159) The echoes of
Morris's aims in Cambridgeshire are distinct but the Committee felt a
broader strategy was needed than just a college - the simple physical
juxtaposition of school, library, hall and adult education centre which
Morris envisaged. What the Committee did not realise was that
financial stringency could convert a publicly-funded policy of
equalisation into a tendency to accentuate differences between villages.

The Scott Report also aired another concern and this was about the
spread of sporadic building in the countryside.

"The suburban spread of houses and factories has been
accentuated by the construction of other buildings - or, it
would be truer to say, by other erections, for many of the
ramshackle creations which so often serve as 'Wayside Cafes',
snack-bars, filling stations and such like, cannot properly
claim the dignity of being described as buildings. The
nameless messes, the assemblages of caravans and converted
'buses and encampments which have littered and spoilt many
a once-charming stretch of coast line, lake-side and river-
side, and a hundred other attractive scenes cannot properly
be called villages; but they form more than a passing intrusion
of the town into the country"
                    (Ministry of Planning and Works, 1942 para. 80).

The Report recommended strongly that the experience of sporadic
building in the countryside in the 1930s should not be repeated after
the war not only because of the aesthetic ugliness of much of the
building, but also because of the harm done to the beauty of the
rural scene by a scattering of new buildings and the social isolation
and unhappiness induced by living away from a village. Consequently,
they recommended that new buildings, especially houses, be put in
towns and villages and not, save in exceptional circumstances, in the
open countryside. This concentration of settlement would save farmland
and make cheaper the provision of public utilities - such provision
being a principal but very costly recommendation of the Report. The
expansion of villages should also be 'as compact as the requirements
of healthy living will permit' (para. 205) - again an echo of Morris's
belief in the beneficial effects of proximity. The close-knit
character of villages was to be preserved by filling in gaps in the
village rather than by it expanding at the edge. This was effectively
the same recommendation as that given in 1937 by the Ministry of

of Health and in 1950 by the Ministry of Town and Country Planning.
It forms one element in the concentration of the rural population.

After 1945, however, most official interest in settlement sizes was
directed further up the hierarchy than the single settlement. The
smaller villages and hamlets also became the focus for critical comment.
A view gained currency that not all villages could or should survive
and that the only way public services could be improved to the ever-
rising urban standards without excessive expenditure was by a concerted scheme of discriminating between settlements (Edwards, 1971).
One of the main economic bases for such discrimination was evidence
that there existed economies of scale in the provision of public
services. It was argued that it was cheaper to provide one large
school, library or sewage works than several smaller ones, from which
developed the policy of deliberately concentrating the provision of
public facilities.

Such a policy was vigorously pursued in the Soviet Union and the
work of the architect, N.S. Smirnov in 1961 purported to show how
service provision became more expensive as village size was reduced
(Pallot, 1979 p.217). His work provided data to support on economic
grounds the policy of population concentration which had been pursued
for a decade on grounds of equity. Mr. Khrushchev had been an
enthusiastic supporter of this ever since his ill-fated espousal of
the 'agrotown' in the early 1950s (Frankland, 1966 pp.82-6). Altruism,
ideology and preventing urban migration all demanded higher rural
standards and Smirnov's work suggested larger rural settlements could
achieve this at minimum cost. In Great Britain, a study in the North
Walsham area of Norfolk showed that a concentration of services would
cost less to build and was a much cheaper system to run (Cloke, 1979
pp.31-2).

Recently this economies-of-scale argument has been challenged on two
grounds. The first is the argument that while dispersal may be costly,
it does provide a better standard of service. This argument is
frequently used with respect to small country schools where discipline
and staff-pupil ratios are said to be superior leading to more effective learning. Against this it may be contended that small schools
offer a narrower range of subjects and their quality of instruction
depends critically on the few teachers available. One bad teacher in
a two-teacher school can be disastrous for the whole school whereas in
a larger school steps can be taken to minimise the harm done.

It was also questioned whether the cheapness of a concentrated pattern
of services is real or just a product of incomplete accounting. In the
U.S.S.R. economists and geographers challenged the savings claimed for
concentration by the architects and town planners (Pallot, 1979 p.219).
Kovalev, a geographer, noted in the late 1960s how concentration would
reduce the productivity of agriculture because of poorer supervision
of workers and more time wasted travelling between house and field.
In 1975 two economists, Beln'ky and Krants, also questioned Smirnov's
figures by extending his analysis to include the cost of the phased

introduction of new services (costs which rose with size of settlement)
and also the costs of longer commuting, the expense of removals and
the expenditure needed in the short term to keep minimum levels of
service in the 'non-viable' settlements until they were completely
closed. They argued that account should also be taken of the food lost
from private plots fewer of which would be cultivated since the workers
lived further away from them. With this broader analysis, the economic
case for concentration was much less convincing than it was made to
appear in the 1960s and the policy of increasing the size of rural
settlements in the U.S.S.R. is now pursued much less vigorously.

In the United Kingdom a study by Gilder in 1979 of the Bury St.
Edmunds district of Suffolk has produced similar results by measuring
costs and benefits as fully as possible. Although Gilder found marked
internal economies of scale in the provision of fixed services such as
education and sewerage, the size of settlement was not very important
in explaining variations in the cost of providing services with a
detectable tendency for unit costs of provision to rise with increasing
settlement size. The cheapest strategy for accommodating extra
population (rather than starting from scratch) was to expand all
existing settlements rather than concentrate growth in the larger ones.
Any benefits from concentrating service provision were outweighed by
the lower marginal cost of using existing facilities more fully.
However, Gilder's conclusions do not yet represent conventional wisdom
in the United Kingdom which is currently better expressed in the
Treasury's Rural Depopulation. This viewed rural service provision as
35 per cent more expensive than the national average.

"Another implication is that the additional costs of providing
services and infrastructure in small towns must be accepted as
part of the cost of preventing depopulation. This raises the
question whether there is some minimum size for a viable
community in rural areas. Many efforts have been made to
define the minimum viable community; but viability is an
elusive concept and it is difficult to put numbers to it.
Clearly the size of the viable community depends on what
services people require; and as standards rise in all sorts
of spheres - schooling, medical care, sanitation, shopping,
entertainments - the size of community which provides the
minimum of services which most people think essential gets
larger."
(H.M. Treasury, 1976 pp.20-1).

The concept of viability may be elusive, it may depend on personal
mobility and the level of public transport but it is nonetheless a
valid concept in the Treasury's eyes and one which implies a cost to
the Exchequer. Its vulnerability to cuts in public expenditure is
obvious and even rational in these terms. The economic argument
against population concentration is not yet fully developed and further
research to clarify the issue is needed.

The key settlement policy pursued in Britain and elsewhere has not

only drawn strength from the arguments about savings in the cost of
service provision but also from a variant of growth pole theory. It
is contended that if the growth of population is concentrated spatially,
then the rapidly expanding villages will attract new shops and industry
with linkages developing between local firms. More employment will
be generated and more income retained in the local economy by a
concentrated settlement pattern than by a dispersed one.

These arguments derive from François Perroux's conception of the
growth pole but only loosely since Perroux envisaged not only a spatial
concentration but also a sectoral specialisation. The growth pole
justification for key settlement policy derives solely from the
spatial concentration. The principal difficulties with using growth
pole theory usefully in the context of urban areas and regional policy
have been the problems of identifying the best areas and sectors of
the economy. The choice of the latter has largely been ignored in
rural planning which has concerned itself with total population and
services. The choice of the places for growth has been more careful
but scarcely more secure. It is not clear, for example, how many
growth centres a given area should have (Moseley, 1973). Central
Scotland had eight growth centres in 1965 while all of Spain had only
seven (Buttler, 1975). The choice of centres for expansion has often
been conducted on the basis of the existing total population.
Settlements over a given threshold of population were designated for
expansion while smaller ones were not, unless they performed an
important function in the settlement pattern or there were no other
growth centres nearby. Not surprisingly, key settlements have been
chosen with reference to population thresholds ranging between 250
and 1,000 people in different rural areas. Whether this is sympto-
matic of a chronic theoretical weakness in all aspects of the policy
or rather is a sound recognition of the geographical variability of
settlement patterns, growth potential and transport systems is a moot
point.

The other difficulty with the economic arguments for a key settlement
policy lies in the application of a static policy to a very fluid
economy. The thresholds for the sale of goods and the variable cost
of travel can alter the minimum size of hinterland for shops and
public services as the experience of planners in the Dutch polders
shows (Clout, 1972 p.150). In 1954 the intention was to provide the
East Flevoland polder with a regional centre, a middle-order centre
and ten villages. By 1965 this had been reduced to a regional and a
middle-order centre and two villages. The degree of personal mobility
had changed rapidly and this Dutch example is just one demonstration of
its spatial consequences.

At this point it is necessary to widen the discussion. The principal
objection to a key settlement policy has long been social rather than
economic. While it is not doubted that the motive for such a policy
was laudable - raising rural living standards at minimum cost to the
community - there is concern over whether key settlement policy will
achieve this in practice. The policy will not automatically raise

everyone's living standards. The population of the key settlements
will benefit from the policy as will those outside the key settlements
who have access to a form of transport which is cheap for their size
of family and at times of the day convenient for their purpose
(hospital visiting, for example). All rural communities have those
who do not have a car or who can only afford one by spending less on
other things. The young, the old, the infirm, wives with children
and the poor may all have a markedly poorer standard of living as
facilities are centralised and effectively move further away from
them. They can, of course, leap-frog over the key settlement and
migrate to the towns where the lack of a car will be less of a
handicap. Yet key settlement policy was originally designed to stop
urban migration and it does nothing to provide housing for rural
migrants in the towns. The countryside outside the key settlements is
then left to those who can afford to live there and those who have to,
whatever the cost. Ironically, public transport has tended to
deteriorate as services have been withdrawn on the same cost-cutting
grounds as the pub, shop, school and cottage hospital. The dilemma of
migrating or having a lower standard of living has become more acute
for those without a car as reduced public transport and fewer services
in non-key villages have coincided with rising expectations.

The arguments against a key settlement policy have been strengthened
by the way the policy has been implemented. When a local council with
a political inclination against spending money was presented with a
rationale for spending less, the acceptance of key settlement policy
was almost inevitable. Cloke has noted how the selection of key
settlements in Devon and Warwickshire was either influenced by
political power or was based on little more than the population of the
settlement, itself partly a reflection of past planning decisions.
The policy was often not strictly enforced while the backlog of
previous planning permissions allowed growth in non-key settlements.
Conversely, where growth was allowed it was often frustrated by
inadequate water supply or sewage capacity. Key settlement policy was
not able to co-ordinate the investment plans of the many branches of
local and national government. When key settlement policy has been
used in an urbanised county such as Warwickshire it has often proved
difficult to refuse all the many requests for planning permission for
new houses in non-key settlements. Yet the key settlements in Devon
had received only 22.5 per cent of the new houses in the county by
1970 and had had only an average rate of population growth. By 1974
half the key settlements could not expand because of limited sewage
facilities (Gilg, 1978 p.115). The extreme extension of the policy is
to demolish completely some villages which are deemed not to be viable
but this is an expensive and politically difficult operation. County
Durham succeeded in completely removing eight villages by 1970 but
since then they have been much more cautious with this sort of policy
(Clout, 1972 p.152). Cumberland designated some villages for no
development but then had to upgrade some mining villages in the west
of the county when they showed unexpected signs of vitality. This
changing of policy does call into question the perspicacity of the
original classification of settlements' growth potential.

The policy has also been criticised for its tendency to polarise
the social composition of the non-key settlements. If the supply of
houses in some villages is virtually fixed, their price will tend to
rise as people from the cities look for country properties. The less
mobile will move out and the more affluent will move in, creating
the rural equivalent of the gentrification of parts of our cities.
The balance of advantage is difficult to measure since one has to set
a rather nebulous loss of 'community' against the free market in
housing and the improvement to old property carried out by the newcomers. A study of changes in the social composition of villages in
north Norfolk and south Nottinghamshire by Parsons (1977) illustrates
the difficulties of this debate however. While it is possible to
show that there has been an increase in the proportion of a village's
population who are in certain socio-economic classes (professional and
managerial groups, for example), it is not clear that their arrival
has diminished the standard of living of those who formerly occupied
the houses. Nor is it at all clear how one should measure social
change. With what should the present social composition be compared
so as to establish social polarisation? Evans (1981) observed that
there had been social polarisation in non-key settlements in
Leicestershire but that this process had started before key settlement
policy and did not seem to have been greatly intensified by it. In
addition there is the problem of the counterfactual. The social
composition of the village might have been similarly altered without
key settlement policy given that rural outmigration, long distance
commuting and the buying of cottages as second homes or for retirement are all trends of much longer standing than key settlement policy.

Even if the policy of concentrating housing and public facilities
has not worked as rapidly or rationally as intended, it clearly has
worked to some extent despite the lack of public awareness of the
policy (Cloke, 1979 p.226 and pp.196-8). The concentration of
population in key settlements has outstripped the attraction of new
jobs and surpassed our ability to make the benefits of life in the
key settlements available to their hinterland. The Development
Commissioners have attempted to attract industry to the larger
villages and smaller towns by providing small advanced factories but
this has not been properly co-ordinated with housing policy nor on a
sufficient scale.

Key settlement policy illustrates a number of the more common
difficulties which beset rural planning in Great Britain. The work
of planners is not adequately co-ordinated with that of other
departments of local and central government nor with the investment
policies of the agencies providing infrastructure. The lack of co-
ordination with public and private house builders is particularly
unfortunate since neither planning nor housing policy can be effectively pursued independently of the other. Rural planning also relies
heavily on negative planning control, that is, the right to refuse
permission for developments which do not conform to the plan. If
there are too few applications for developments which conform to the
plan, there is little the planning authority can do to promote growth.

County planning departments have no automatic control over the housing policy of the district councils, for example. Rural planning generally, like key settlement policy in particular, has a very weak theoretical basis and, what theory there is, was seized eagerly as justification for policy. The lack of theoretical guidance may have contributed to the many variants by key settlement policy which have been used in different situations and in many different ways. There was also an inadequate definition of the character of the countryside desired in preference to that which would evolve from a situation without planning.

A further characteristic is the way policy is justified in what planners see (perhaps incorrectly) as economic terms while social concerns are given limited attention. Such economic goals as there are tend to be macro-economic in the sense of being concerned with total expenditure rather than setting out to achieve welfare objectives. The distribution in society of the costs and benefits of rural planning policy is rarely considered explicitly yet both a welfare and an expenditure approach need to be used, irrespective of what decision is eventually made. Key settlement policy was perhaps over-sold, being used in areas as different as those with depopulation and those with severe urban pressures. While this policy, like most others in rural planning, started out with laudable intentions - raising rural living standards as efficiently as possible - it gave too little attention to evaluating other options for achieving this. This may be because the alternatives were not clearly planning strategies and so were less readily considered by planning departments. The administrative fragmentation at local and national levels between planning and housing is indefensible except on grounds of organisational convenience, yet its consequences are a recurring theme in the history of the British countryside.

The study of the recent controversies over key settlement policy and tied cottages highlights three general features of the relationship between planning and housing in the countryside. First, some problems reach an impasse and only changing circumstances, new priorities or a different way of conceptualizing the problem will allow the conflict to be resolved. Delay may not only be expedient but a genuinely useful tool of planning. Second, planning the countryside must consider who lives where but it is not self-evident that land-use planning can always improve any deficiencies identified in housing supply. Third, while planning must consider many factors in any given housing problem, it is often expedient to allow one factor to dominate the decision-making - the alleged cost of service provision in key settlement policy and the needs of farmers in the tied cottage debate, for example.

The relationship between housing and planning in the Lake District will now be considered in detail to illustrate problems and potentials more clearly.

4. Housing and Planning in the Lake District

'Monday 9th (June 1800). In the morning W. cut the winter cherry
tree. I sowed French beans and weeded. A coronetted Landau went
by, when we were sitting upon the sodded wall. The ladies
(evidently Tourists) turned an eye of interest upon our little
garden and cottage.'

Dorothy Wordsworth. Grasmere Journal.

4.1 INTRODUCTION

The Lake District is the upland area of north-west England, centred
on the highest mountains in England and lying between Morecambe Bay
and the Solway Firth (Figure 5). It is an ideal area in which to
study the relationship between rural housing and planning because it
is a microcosm of the features of so many other parts of the British
countryside. It has witnessed depopulation in some areas and in
others considerable in-migration and pressure from townspeople. It
has experienced many of the trends and conflicts in rural housing in
particular. In addition, the Lake District is perhaps the best known
national park in Great Britain. National parks were a post-war
addition to planning which were to provide special planning for ten
distinctive areas of coastline and upland countryside in England and
Wales. The problems and pressures in the Lake District National Park
provide a testing environment in which to examine how this part of
British planning has performed. It will allow us to see the
priorities planning authorities have adopted and which options they
have pursued to reach their objectives.

The Lake District has always been regarded as a special area,
different from the rest of England in its dialect, the Viking
influence on its settlement and place names, and a ruggedness of
topography not found elsewhere in England combined with twelve major
lakes. The scenic beauty and grandeur of the area aroused awe in the
eighteenth century.

'Here, among the mountains, our curiousity was frequently moved to
enquire what high hill this was, or that. Indeed, they were, in my
thoughts, monstrous high. Nor were these hills high and formidable
only, but they had a kind of unhospitable terror in them. Here
were no rich pleasant valleys between them, as among the Alps; no
lead mines and veins of rich ore, as in the Peak; no coal pits, as
in the hills about Hallifax, much less gold, as in the Andes, but
all barren and wild, of no use or advantage either to man or beast
(...) This part of the country yields little or nothing at all
(...)

50

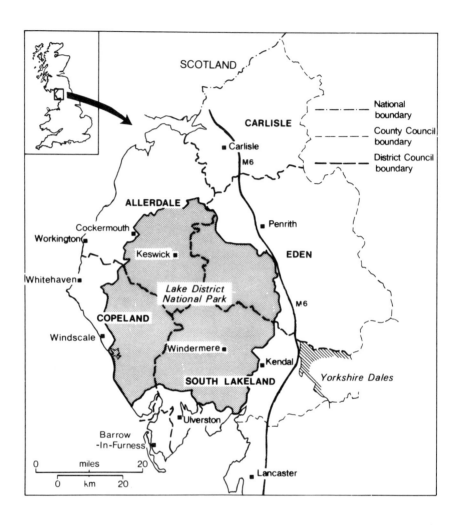

FIG.5. The Lake District.

Here we entered Westmoreland, a country eminent only for
being the wildest, most barren and frightful of any that I have
passed over in England, or even in Wales it self; the west
side, which borders on Cumberland, is indeed bounded by a chain
of almost unpassable mountains, which, in the language of the
country, are called Fells (...)'
Daniel Defoe. A Tour through the Whole Island of Great Britain
(1724-27).

By the nineteenth century the area had come to epitomise natural
beauty as this passage from Wordsworth's Guide to the Lake shows

'I will take this opportunity of observing, that they who have
studied the appearances of Nature feel that the superiority,
in point of visual interest, of mountainous over other countries
- is more strikingly displayed in winter than in summer. This
is partly owing to the greater variety that exists in their
winter than their summer colouring. The oak-coppices, upon
the sides of the mountains, retain russet leaves; the birch
stands conspicuous with its silver stem and puce-coloured twigs;
the hollies, with green leaves and scarlet berries, have come
forth to view from among the deciduous trees, whose summer
foliage had concealed them; the ivy is now plentifully apparent
upon the stems and boughs of the trees, and upon the steep
rocks. In place of the deep summer-green of the herbage and
fern, many rich colours play into each other over the surface
of the mountains; turf (the tints of which are interchangeably
tawny-green, olive and brown), beds of withered fern, and grey
rocks, being harmoniously blended together. The mosses and
lichens are never so fresh and flourishing as in winter, if
it be not a season of frost; and their minute beauties
prodigally adorn the foreground (...) to the observing passenger,
their forms and colours are a source of inexhaustible admiration.'
William Wordsworth. Guide to the Lakes (1835).

Numerous literary associations with Wordsworth, Coleridge,
de Quincey, Southey and later John Ruskin and Beatrix Potter served
to multiply the area's admirers (Cosgrove 1979). Indeed it is
arguable that the Lakeland landscape is popularly viewed in terms
of Wordsworthian beauty as much as in terms of what is to be found
today. It is now invested with such a wealth of meaning that it
is hard to view it afresh (Lowenthal and Prince 1965 p.195). By
the time the railway network had encircled the Lake District and
penetrated into Keswick and Windermere, the area's attractiveness
for tourists was firmly established and this has never been lost.

However, the Lake District is not a very promising area for
settlement. About half of it is over 250 metres in altitude and
rainfall can be over 3,000mm a year in the wettest areas. Even this
was turned to advantage in early guide books which recommended
visiting the Lakes in the wet months since 'roving vapors (sic) gave
the landscape a luminous softness most like a wash drawing or

52

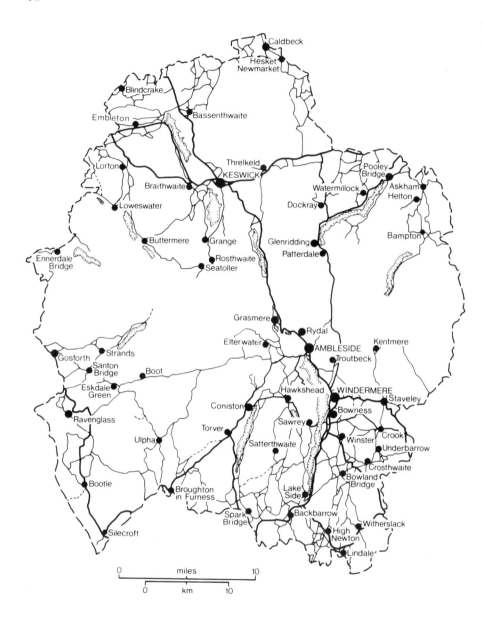

FIG.6.   Settlement pattern in the Lake District (after L.D.S.P.B.,
          1978).

aquatint' (Lowenthal and Prince 1965 p.195). The Solway Plain and
the north shore of Morecambe Bay are much drier but the central
Lake District is definitely wet as many a tourist in August knows
only too well. Yet there are rich soils derived from loess in the
south and even in the dales such as Borrowdale and Hartsop the soils
on the valley bottoms can be quite fertile. It is a difficult
landscape to farm but not a poor one if the right crops and animals
are raised skilfully. The settlement pattern of the Lake District
is surprisingly dense given how little lowland there is in most
areas (Figure 6). There are no large towns and economically the
area is divided into the hinterlands of the surrounding towns of
Barrow, Whitehaven, Carlisle and Kendal (Figure 7).

The area is also similar to many other upland areas in being
dominated by a few large landowners. Cadastral information in
Britain is not easy to map but Figure 8 shows that public bodies
such as the Forestry Commission, National Trust and North West Water
Authority own 29 per cent of the Park much of which is also common
land. The Water Authority took over the land formerly belonging to
Manchester Corporation which bought the Thirlmere estate soon after
1879. The National Trust, founded in 1895, first acquired land in
the Lake District at Brandlehow Woods, Derwentwater, in 1902, and
is now the largest landowner in the Lake District owning 32,000
hectares mostly in central Lakeland. However from the point of view
of settlement, their control of land is less dominant than it might
seem since their holdings tend to comprise the higher land. In
the valleys and the lowlands surrounding the hills, smaller private
landowners became dominant. The largest are the Lowther Estates
centred on Penrith and with land extending to 29,150 hectares and
including some land in West Cumbria where their holdings were once
extensive and included iron ore workings near Millom and the town
of Whitehaven. Through their holding company, Lakeland Investment,
they also own land in Langdale and Grasmere as well as around
Penrith. Employing 210 people directly in 1976 and with 90 tenant
farms, they are a major supplier of housing. Through a Housing
Association they have built new houses on the eastern edge of the
Park and have restored and modernised James Adam's Lowther village.
The estate used to own whole villages but much property has been
sold. The large private estate and the medium-sized and large farms
were formerly the most important providers of rented accommodation
in the Park but, as owner-occupation and public housing have
expanded in scope, their influence has waned. Changes in farming
have also had an effect on housing. Between 1963 and 1975 there was
a decline of over a quarter in the number of farms in the Lake
District and one-fifth fewer farm workers were employed while
estates have also sold off surplus housing. The National Trust,
which owns 78 small farms has adopted a more cautious policy towards
expanding or amalgamating their farms, nonetheless the growth of
public policy as an influence on housing has been as remarkable as
it has been in so many other aspects of Lakeland life.

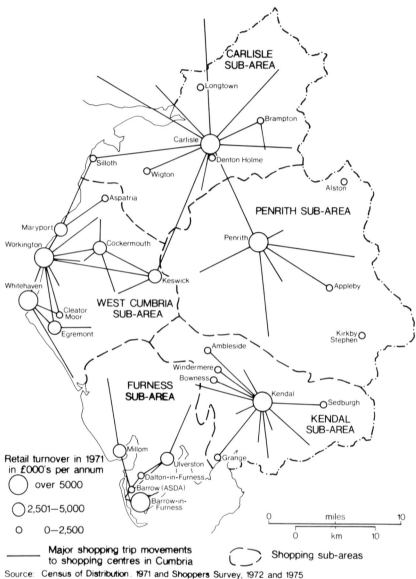

FIG.7.   Functional areas in Cumbria - pattern of shopping in 1971
         (after C.C.C. and L.D.S.P.B., 1976).

One means by which public policy has been brought to bear has been through the establishment of a National Park in the area of the Lake District. This has had a major impact on housing in the area both directly and also indirectly through the assumptions and values implicit in national park status in Great Britain. Often these attitudes are of long-standing and have their origins in the inter-war period before the Park was established.

In the 1930s the major local controversy, which by 1936 had done so much to weld together the disparate groups seeking to protect the Lake District, was the role of forestry in the area. On the one side was the Forestry Commission which bought upland estates cheaply given the depressed state of farming and afforested them. The Commission was always in danger from the Treasury seeking to reduce government expenditure, but in the 1930s it acquired powerful allies for its potential role in alleviating the severe unemployment on the West Cumbrian coalfield and so the Special Areas Afforestation Scheme included the Lake District. Afforestation of the Lake District was therefore supported both for its strategic role in creating a reserve of timber and for its creation of jobs. On the other side of a debate which became increasingly polarised were the opponents of state forestry who saw conifers as incompatible with the open fells and the mixed broad-leaved trees of the dales. It must be admitted that much of the Forestry Commission's work was crude in terms of landscape design with straight rows of a single species imposed on a subtle landscape. The Commission were not averse to granting public access to their forests and in 1936 they established their first National Forest Park in Argyllshire.

The particular incident which sparked off the immediate controversy was the Commission's purchase, on very favourable terms, of the Hardknott estate in the western dales. Sandbach (1978) has described the detailed manoeuvrings in the case and has identified the key role of the Friends of the Lake District pressure group in securing a concordat with the Commission on forestry in the National Park. The position of the Friends of the Lake District is set out neatly by Symonds in Afforestation in the Lake District (1936) where he details the mixture of argument and emotion which comprised the opposition to coniferous plantations.

The final agreement was a compromise (Figure 9). The Forestry Commission conceded that no new forestry should take place in the core of the Lake District but the size of the core was reduced during negotiations with the Commission from 1088 sq.km. to 770 sq.km. In addition, other areas outside this core were to be the subject of detailed consultation before planting could be allowed. Since the National Park was established, the central core has remained inviolate except for two small areas near Loweswater which were wooded in 1936 and have been restocked after felling, while further peripheral areas have been added to the area for consul-tation (Figure 10). In Area 1 small scale planting of mixed species was envisaged while in Areas 2A and 2B only minor planting will be

56

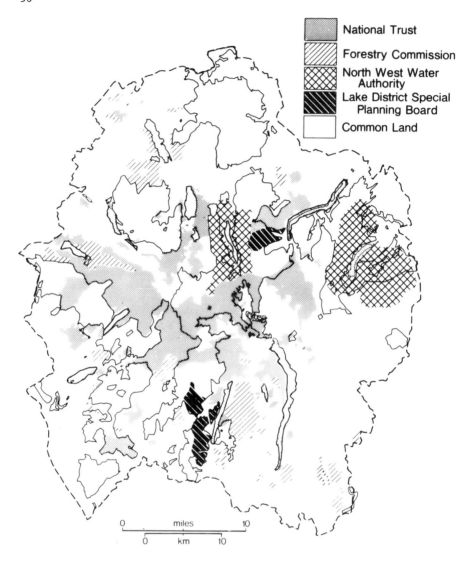

National Trust

Forestry Commission

North West Water
Authority

Lake District Special
Planning Board

Common Land

0   miles   10

0   km   10

FIG.8.   Landownership in the Lake District (after L.D.S.P.B., 1978).

allowed if it helps farming or improves the landscape. In Area 3 a
fairly tolerant view of forestry, including large scale forestry,
would be taken. Since only 40 per cent of the woodland in the Park
was owned by the Forestry Commission and 34 per cent by other public
bodies including the National Trust, it was felt essential to include
private landowners in the control of forestry. A committee
representing the National Park, the Country Landowners Association
and the Timber Growers Organisation was set up in 1962 to advise on
planting by private landowners so that this might concur with the aims
of landscape protection. Although this planning control is voluntary
and not statutory, it highlights the extent of the concern for
maintaining the landscape in all national parks and particularly in
the Lake District. The aim of maintaining the visual status quo,
started before a National Park was declared in the Lake District, has
continued since in many spheres, including housing, reinforced, as
before, by the arguments of pressure groups such as Friends of the
Lake District.

The belief that the particular qualities of the Lake District could
only be preserved from harm through the imposition of some national
body to protect the area in the national interest is not a new one.

'It is then much to be wished that a better taste should prevail
among these new proprietors; and, as they cannot be expected to
leave things to themselves, that skill and knowledge should
prevent unnecessary deviations from that path of simplicity and
beauty along which, without design and unconsciously, their
humble predecessors have moved. In this wish the author will be
joined by persons of pure taste throughout the whole island, who,
by their visits (often repeated) to the Lakes in the North of
England, testify that they deem the district a sort of national
property, in which every man has a right and interest who has an
eye to perceive and a heart to enjoy.'
                 William Wordsworth A Guide to the Lakes (1835)

A National Park for the Lake District was established in 1951 to
carry out the duties and responsibilities of the National Parks and
Access to the Countryside Act of 1949 (Ch. 97). This stated that
national parks were "for the purpose of preserving and enhancing the
natural beauty of the areas specified in the next following subsection; and for the purpose of promoting their enjoyment by the
public" (S5 (1)). The national park authorities were also to have
regard to the economic and social well-being of the area (S84). It
was quickly realised that these aims were potentially conflicting
particularly regarding agriculture, forestry and tourist development
but only later did it become apparent that planning for housing
would also be complicated by these conflicting duties.

The body charged with carrying out these functions was the Lake
District Planning Board which became the Lake District Special
Planning Board when local government was reorganised in England and
Wales in 1974. Its detailed policies for the Park were set out in

58

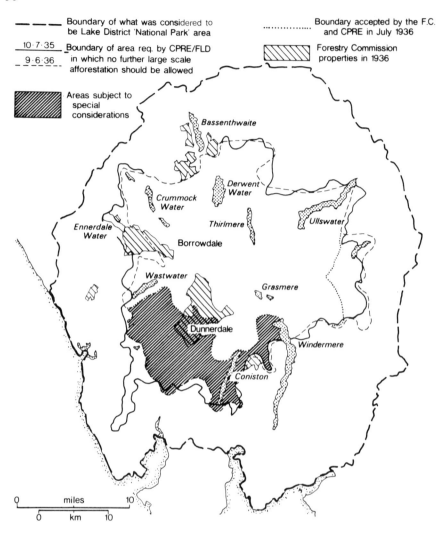

FIG.9.   The 1936 afforestation agreement in the Lake District
          (after Sandbach, 1978).

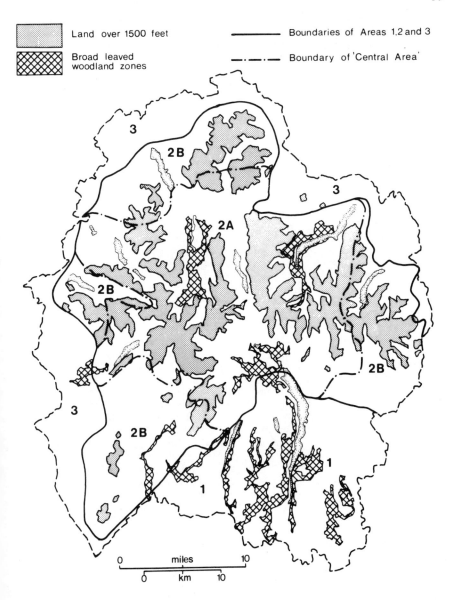

Land over 1500 feet

Broad leaved
woodland zones

Boundaries of Areas 1,2 and 3

Boundary of 'Central Area'

FIG.10.   Forest and woodland policy in the Lake District National
           Park (after L.D.S.P.B., 1978).

the Development Plan of 1956, which was amended in 1965, and then in the National Park Plan of 1978 and the Joint Structure Plan of 1980, the latter needing the approval of the Secretary of State for the Environment. The Special Planning Board is comprised of members two-thirds of whom are nominated by Cumbria County Council and one-third of whom are appointed by the Secretary of State for the Environment who also provides 75 per cent of the Board's funds.

4.2   GENERAL NEED FOR COUNCIL HOUSING

Initially the Planning Board was not particularly concerned with housing since the direct provision of housing was a function of borough and district councils. The Board's main concern was with the landscape and its protection from unsuitable and unsightly development. The Lake District, like all areas, has its poorer people who cannot afford to buy a house. Traditionally low-wage industries such as agriculture, forestry, and work in hotels, catering and shops have accounted for a larger proportion of the workforce than elsewhere. In 1971 farming employed 13.9 per cent of the employed people in the Lake District compared with 6.8 per cent in Cumbria and 2.0 per cent in England and Wales. The service sector is also over-represented in the area compared with other areas (Cumbria C.C., 1976 p.75). In the Kendal employment exchange area 60 per cent of the work force are in services and in the Keswick area 75 per cent are so employed, compared with 56 per cent for Great Britain as a whole. The retailing, hotel and catering sectors of the service sector are traditionally areas of low average wages. Although some lower-paid employees are supplied with accommodation by hotel owners and farmers, many are not, particularly on retirement. In addition many workers have low incomes although measurement of the spatial variation of incomes is not easy. A variety of sources confirm that the average income in Cumbria is less than the national average although the gap has been closing. According to Inland Revenue data, the net income per tax case in 1959/60 in Cumberland was only 94 per cent of the U.K. average and in 1970/71 it was 97 per cent. In Westmorland the corresponding figures were 104 per cent and 95 per cent. The New Earnings Survey of 1974 again showed that for Cumbria income was lower than the England and Wales average (Table 3) even before allowance is made for absence due to sickness which is higher in the Northern Region (Cumbria C.C., 1976 pp. 82-3).

A more detailed survey of total household income in Cumbria revealed wide variations between the parishes, some having incomes far above the county average and some far below it (Figure 11). These parish figures are themselves averages, which will conceal even wider extremes of income. Of course income is only a part of the story since this has to be set against the cost of living in rural areas which is itself a function of patterns of consumption and prices. Detailed information on the cost of living in the Lake District is not available but surveys in rural Scotland in 1979 and 1980 showed that the cost of living in rural Scotland was about 10 per cent higher than in Aberdeen which was the city chosen as a reference point. Food prices were about 9.8 per cent higher, consumer durables 18 per cent dearer and housing 7 per cent dearer.

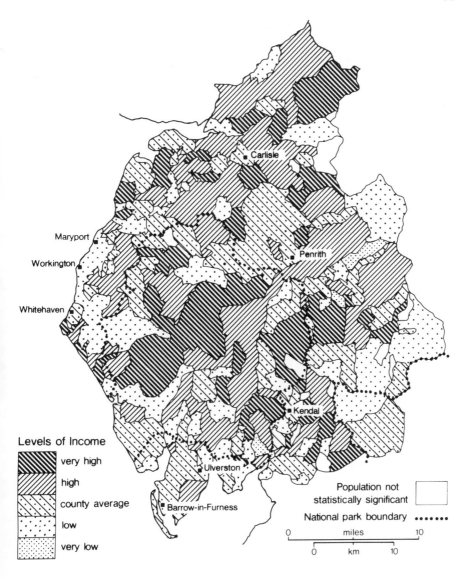

Levels of Income

very high

high

county average

low

very low

Population not
statistically significant

National park boundary ⬤⬤⬤⬤⬤⬤

Carlisle

Maryport

Workington

Whitehaven

Penrith

Kendal

Ulverston

Barrow-in-Furness

0   miles   10

0   km   10

FIG.11.   Estimated mean household income in Cumbria (after C.C.C.
           and L.D.S.P.B., 1976).

62

TABLE 3. Average Gross Weekly Earnings, 1974*

	Cumbria	North Region	England and Wales
Full-time manual workers over 21	£41.2	£43.6	£43.7
% of above earning less than £40	50.6	42.3	43.5
All full-time male workers over 21	£44.9	£46.2	£47.9
% of above earning less than £40	45.3	39.3	38.5
All full-time female workers over 18	£24.9	£25.5	£27.1
% of above earning less than £25	58.0	56.7	50.7

*Based on cases where pay is not affected by absence.

Source: New Earnings Survey and Cumbria C.C. (1976) p.82.

TABLE 4. Activity rates.

| | Men | Women | |
| | | Single, Widowed or Divorced | Married |
Travel-to-work area	%	%	%
Kendal	77.8	40.3	41.7
Keswick	74.4	38.3	42.1
Ulverston	78.8	35.9	38.8
Grange-over-Sands	67.7	28.3	34.4
Cumbria	80.3	40.7	39.8
Great Britain	81.4	43.4	42.4

Source: 1971 Census and Cumbria County Council (1976) p.70.

TABLE 5. Size of waiting lists for council houses.

| | Waiting List | | No. of council |
	Households	People	houses
Allerdale	457	903	608
Eden	49	121	120
Copeland	65	151	84
S. Lakeland	648	1276	1357
TOTAL	1219	2451	2169

Transport and service costs were slightly lower in the rural areas but, overall, higher prices in the Scottish countryside had to be met from lower incomes. This conclusion did not take account of unemployment rates which are usually lower in rural areas and in November 1978 were 2.8 percentage points below the Great Britain average in Kendal and 0.8 per cent lower in Keswick. On the other hand, the proportion of men and women in work in rural areas also tends to be lower as Table 4 shows. For those who do not work, incomes will probably be lower than the figures in the surveys quoted earlier which were all based on people in full employment.

Many of the jobs taken by married women in the Kendal and Keswick areas are of course seasonal jobs in the tourist industry, while the figures for the Grange area are unusually low even by the standards of Cumbria due to the town's popularity as a retirement area.

There are some wealthy people in the Lake District - some work there and some have retired there. But there are also many families whose income, even allowing for working wives, is too low to contemplate house purchase or to afford an open-market rent. These are the people for whom council housing is designed and their numbers are increased by the elderly, the unemployed and the chronically sick.

4.3 PROVISION OF COUNCIL HOUSING IN THE LAKE DISTRICT

Public housing represents the obvious solution to the housing needs of the lower-income sections of the community yet there is less council housing in rural Cumbria than in most other parts of the country. In 1979, only 12 per cent of housing stock of the Lake District National Park were council houses compared with 21 per cent in rural England as a whole in 1971, 28 per cent in England generally and 52 per cent in rural Scotland. Some forty per cent of the new houses built in the National Park between 1951 and 1976 were council houses and these 2000 new houses increased the number of council houses in the Park nearly ten-fold (Lake District Special Planning Board, 1978, p.151). Even in the period 1967-73 when council house building was generally rapid, the number of new council houses per head of population in the central Cumbrian area was under half the English and Welsh average (Shucksmith, 1981 p.69), and Figure 7 reinforces this point in more detail. The Lakeland district councils also receive below average grants per capita for public housing (Shucksmith, 1981 p.125). Yet the provision of council houses poses great problems for a local authority since difficult decisions have to be taken on how many new council houses should be built and where they should be sited. This requires a careful study of the concept of the demand for housing before the current situation can be assessed.

There are two components which make up the concept of demand for housing. The first is the volume of demand - how many people need a council house - and the second is the urgency of demand, that is the severity of their need for a council house.

   Since there is, as yet, no open market in council houses, the assessment of demand and the subsequent scale of provision can only be ascertained through a study of the waiting lists of the District Councils. These lists record all who have applied for a council house and have not yet been allocated one. The lists are sometimes criticised for this type of research on the grounds that they record a demand for council houses which is inflated by the inclusion of people who apply for a house even though they are already adequately housed. They may, for example, wish to have a house of a different size or they may want a house nearer town or nearer their place of work. This point can be met by measuring the degree of need of those on the waiting lists rather than simply accepting without qualification the total number on the list as a fair measure of demand. Conversely the waiting lists exclude those in genuine need of a house who do not apply for one but migrate instead or do not feel it is worth their while applying since they believe they will not get a house. There may be no council houses in their parish as in 38 per cent of the Lake District's parishes and this deters people from applying for a council house. Some people in real need may not be on a waiting list because of a residence qualification such as that used by Copeland District Council in 1978. With these provisos the waiting lists are an adequate basis for a study of housing need. In South Lakeland a 25 per cent sample of those on the waiting list in February 1980 was analysed and all the results presented here have been multiplied by four to give an estimate of the true situation in that district. In other districts a study was made of the complete waiting lists.

   Table 5 shows the number of households and people on each District Council's waiting list for a house in the Park. The lists differ greatly in size depending on whether there is a large town in the district. Thus the Allerdale and South Lakeland lists are longer since these districts include Keswick and Windermere.

   It is also important to know where the applicants wish to live and so Table 6 cross-tabulates for Allerdale and South Lakeland Districts each household's present parish of residence and their desired parish of residence. Table 6 shows how Keswick dominates the pattern for Allerdale District. Not only do just over half the households on the waiting list live there but Keswick attracts applicants from nearly every parish and almost no one living in Keswick wishes a council house anywhere else. The rural applicants form 42 per cent of the households on the Keswick waiting list. Ambleside and Windermere do not dominate the list for South Lakeland District nearly so strongly. The large groups of applicants from outside the Park are drawn disproportionately to Keswick, Ambleside and Windermere. To a very

TABLE 6: Current parish of residence and desired parish for households on waiting lists

| | | First choice parish for council house | | | | | | | | | |
| | | ALLERDALE | | | | | | | | | |
Current Parish of Residence		Un	AD	Bl	Ba	Ca	Ke	Lo	Ir	Bo	TOTAL
	Underskiddaw	3					4				7
	Above Derwent	1	11				29				41
	Blindcrake			4			1				5
	Bassenthwaite				5		3				8
	Caldbeck				1	4			1		6
	Keswick		1		2		229				232
	St. John's etc.		1				19				20
	Lorton							6		1	7
	Ireby						1		1		2
	Embleton						2				2
	Borrowdale						9			2	11
	Setmurthy						1				1
	EDEN		1				4				5
	S. LAKELAND						2				2
	OUTSIDE PARK		6		2	2	97	1			108
	TOTAL	4	20	4	10	6	401	7	2	3	457

TABLE 6. (Continued)

SOUTH LAKELAND

	St	La	Gr	Ha	Co	Am	Wi	W.Br	Ha	Co	U.Al	Cros.*	With.*	TOTAL
Staveley	8						8							16
Langdale		8												8
Grasmere			24			4	4							32
Hawkshead				32	4									36
Coniston					8									8
Ambleside				4		108	8							120
Windermere						16	252							268
W. Broughton					4			8						12
Haverthwaite									8					8
Colton									4		12			4
U. Allithwaite											12			12
Meathop													4	4
Satterthwaite				4				4						4
Kirkby Ireleth									4					4
Blawith										4				4
Lowick								4						4
Keswick						4								4
OUTSIDE PARK	8		8		8	28	40					8		100
TOTAL	16	8	32	40	24	160	312	12	16	4	12	8	4	648

Cros.* = Crosthwaite

With.* = Witherslack

limited extent Patterdale and Threlkeld perform a similar function in
Eden District by attracting applicants from other parishes and from
people living outside the Park. However the commonest pattern of
preference is for a council house in one's current parish of residence which is true of 65 per cent of the households on the waiting
lists in the Park.

The pattern of first choices for a council house has to be
interpreted rather carefully, however. The choices are likely to
represent in part the existing provision of houses as well as people's
unfettered preferences about where they wish to live. In Allerdale
District, for example, the likelihood of obtaining a house is
enhanced if one wishes to live in one's present parish since extra
points are awarded to an applicant for this and the number of points
influences how quickly an applicant will obtain a council house.
Similarly, many applicants in Allerdale District are likely to be
deterred from choosing to live in one of the thirteen Allerdale
parishes which have no council houses. So it is reasonable to assume
that the present distribution of council houses affects the demand for
houses by channelling it into the areas where applicants believe they
have a fair chance of getting a house quickly and by keeping some
people in need off the waiting list altogether. The current
distribution of council houses is shown on Figure 12. However, there
is still some detectable degree of unconstrained preference in the
waiting lists. In Allerdale, for example 97 per cent of the council
houses are in Keswick but only 88 per cent of the households on the
waiting list gave Keswick as their first choice parish. We can
therefore infer some genuine, if modest, desire to continue to live in
smaller settlements. The South Lakeland figures confirm this with
most applicants from the smaller settlements wishing a council house
in their present village.

The current pattern of council housing provision is largely a
function of attitudes and priorities in the past. In what is now
Allerdale District, the former Keswick Urban District Council was an
active provider of council houses while Cockermouth Rural District
Council, which provided houses outside Keswick, concentrated their
house building efforts outside the Park. Similarly, Eden built few
houses in the Park but both Eden and Allerdale Districts as a whole
were active builders of council houses whereas in South Lakeland the
private sector was the more dynamic (Table 7).

However the council house waiting lists are only a fair measure of
the need for housing (and hence of the adequacy of the existing
provision) if this need is defined more carefully. Clearly some
people's need will be greater than others. It is therefore important
to investigate what sort of people are on the waiting list since
young and old will have different housing requirements. Each
applicant household was allocated to one of three classes, namely
single people, families and old-age pensioners. Each of these
categories was subdivided according to whether they were currently
owner-occupiers, tenants or lodgers. As Table 8 shows, single people

68

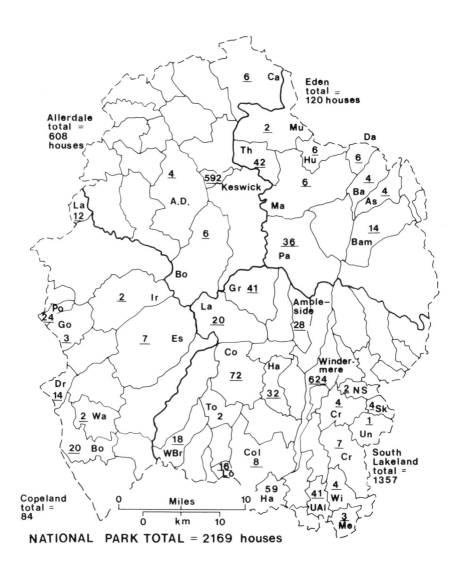

FIG.12.   Number of council houses in the Lake District National
         Park.

TABLE 7. Building Rates: Dwellings Completed (1967-74) Per 1,000
     Population.

District	Public sector	Private sector	Overall
Carlisle	11.8	16.9	28.7
Allerdale	14.8	17.6	32.4
Eden	15.6	20.7	36.2
Copeland	14.5	14.6	29.1
South Lakeland	10.7	54.6	65.3
Barrow	7.7	22.6	30.3
Cumbria	12.3	25.1	37.4
England and Wales	15.2	20.1	35.2

Source: Cumbria C.C. (1976) p.123.

TABLE 8. Status and current housing of households on waiting lists.

	Current Housing			
	Owner-occupier	Tenant	Lodger	TOTAL
Single	1.1%	4.8%	9.0%	14.9%
Family	4.1%	25.2%	14.9%	44.2%
O.A.P.	14.4%	19.4%	7.1%	40.9%
TOTAL	19.6%	49.4%	31.0%	100% = 1219 households

are the smallest category and are principally lodgers. The families
on the list are principally tenants while the pensioners include many
owner-occupiers in Allerdale and Copeland and a considerable number of
tenants, particularly in Eden and South Lakeland.

The figures in Table 8 include 236 households living outside the
Park who are arguably a group of interest in their own right since
they may be distinctive from the rest. About half of them came from
parts of Cumbria outside the Park (Table 9) and a further quarter
come from other counties in northern England. The remainder are
widely dispersed through the United Kingdom.

One may also enquire whether these applicants from outside the Park
are disproportionately drawn from the ranks of the elderly or are
owner-occupiers. Are they perhaps seeking a retirement home in the
Park through the back door, as it were? Both of these assertions
proved to be unfounded since the proportions of owner-occupiers and
pensioners among the applicants are similar for those inside and
outside the Park.

The other principal aspect of the demand for council houses is the
applicant's degree of need for a house. One measure of a household's
need is the number of points allocated to it by the District Housing
Department. However, this is a difficult measure to use in a
comparative study since each district has its own scheme for
awarding points with differing criteria and different weights
attached to the criteria.

Consequently the clerical records about each applicant were studied
and the main reason advanced by the applicant for requiring a council
house was recorded. The results are summarised in Table 10 for all
four districts. The basic unit is the household and not individual
people and the results are shown separately for single people,
families, pensioners and for those living outside the Park. Twenty-
one main reasons for needing a council house emerged with a twenty-
second category for "other reasons". It soon became apparent that
this level of detail was needed if the motives for applying for a
council house were not to be over-simplified or misinterpreted.

Single people need a house principally because they are living with
parents and many of them are intending to marry shortly. Families
need a council house largely because they are living in tied
accommodation or are in a temporary or poor quality house. A
considerable number are also living with their parents. The elderly
have a different and distinctive set of reasons for needing a council
house based largely on poor health or infirmity and a general
inability to cope with large houses and stairs.

The final group comprises those currently living outside the Park
and they have another distinctive and different set of reasons for
needing a council house. Apart from a small group of personnel in
the armed forces, most wish to be nearer family or friends in Cumbria

TABLE 9. Present addresses of applicants living outside the
National Park

	%
Cumbria outside the Park	48.3
Lancashire, Cheshire, Greater Manchester, Merseyside	13.1
N.E. England	6.8
Yorkshire	3.8
Rest of England	20.3
Scotland	3.0
Wales	0.9
Other areas	3.8
TOTAL	100.0% = 236 households

TABLE 10. Major reasons for households being on waiting lists.

Reason	Single	Family	O.A.P.	Outside Park	TOTAL
Tied accommodation	17	85	25	13	140
Living in	41	67	58	9	175
Need cheaper house	-	28	28	1	57
Living in caravan	12	18	9	2	41
Poor health	9	3	46	-	58
Be nearer work	4	9	-	12	25
Present house temporary	10	37	4	6	57
Divorced/separated	5	15	-	-	20
Future marriage and now living in	30	38	-	4	72
O.A.P. can't cope	-	-	139	5	144
Can't use stairs	-	-	38	8	46
Poor housing conditions	-	32	6	-	38
Given notice to quit	9	10	5	4	28
Need more suitable house	-	41	-	9	50
Family separated	-	20	-	1	21
H.M. Forces	1	1	-	15	17
Nearer family/friends	-	1	6	50	57
Return to Cumbria	-	-	-	52	52
Like Cumbria	-	-	-	18	18
Lack of amenities	1	6	8	3	18
Need to be nearer services	-	9	17	8	34
Other reasons	13	18	4	16	51
TOTAL HOUSEHOLDS	152	438	393	236	1219

and most have some past connections with the county. This large
group of applicants experiences to only a limited degree the types of
need given by the other groups.

The families on the waiting list for Allerdale District are more
strongly attracted to a council house in one of the larger towns
than are the single people and old-age pensioners as Table 11 shows.
There is a sufficiently large difference in preferences to require
some explanation, since the two groups have the same pattern of
reasons for needing a council house. Therefore, an analysis was made
of the points awarded to the two groups of families and from this it
seems that the families applying for a house in Keswick have a
slightly greater need for housing since they have an average of $1\frac{1}{2}$
points more than the other families. This is really a small
difference although it might just be interpreted as indicating that
families with a lesser need for housing are more willing and able to
wait the longer period for a rural house to become available.
Families in more urgent need apply for a house in Keswick because
they believe they will get one more quickly there.

4.4 COUNCIL HOUSING PROVISION AND DEMAND

The need for council housing can be put into perspective by
relating it to the existing provision of houses. In Figure 13 the
number of council houses and North Eastern Housing Association
properties in each parish is related to the number of people who are
on the waiting list for a council house in that parish and who are
resident in the Park. Those resident outside the Park give what
might be seen as lower priority reasons for a house (Table 10) and so
they have been excluded from this analysis. Figure 13 shows the
number of years it would take to clear the current waiting list of
locally resident applicants if one were to assume that ten per cent
of the existing stock of council houses in each parish became vacant
each year. If there are fewer than ten council houses in a parish,
one house is assumed to fall vacant each year. If there are no
council houses in the parish, it is assumed that one new house is
built each year. Of course, these assumptions are wholly arbitrary,
but they do allow a ranking of parishes from those where provision
and demand are in balance to those where demand greatly exceeds
provision. If all the assumptions were altered equally to give a
faster or slower rate of turnover of council houses, the number of
years to clear the waiting list would change but the rank order of
the parishes would be the same. Thus the same areas of shortage and
plenty would be identified.

There is in fact a remarkable uniformity of provision and need in
the Park with relatively little spread around the average clearance
time of four years for the whole Park. Copeland and Eden are a
little below this average and Allerdale a little above it. The major
towns of Keswick, Windermere and Ambleside all have average clearance
times and the only areas of clear under-provision are Hawkshead
(where the clearance time is thirteen years) and Gosforth, Grasmere
and Lorton where it is six years.

74

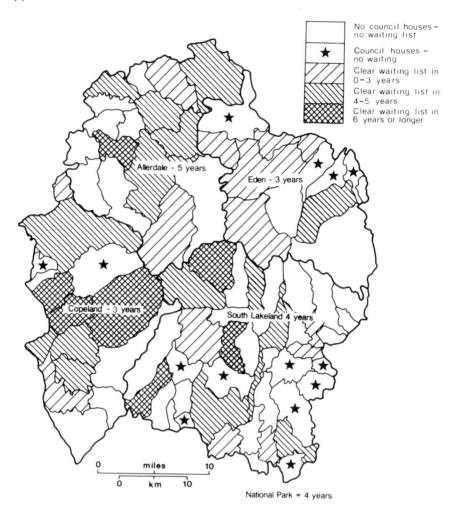

Legend:

- No council houses – no waiting list
- ★ Council houses – no waiting
- Clear waiting list in 0–3 years
- Clear waiting list in 4–5 years
- Clear waiting list in 6 years or longer

Allerdale - 5 years

Eden - 3 years

Copeland - 3 years

South Lakeland 4 years

0   miles   10

0   km   10

National Park = 4 years

FIG.13. Council housing and waiting lists in the Lake District
National Park.

TABLE 11. First preference of Allerdale applicants for a council
house.

Percentage preferring house:

	In Keswick	Outside Keswick
Single people	91.6%	8.4%
Families	70.4%	29.6%
Pensioners	94.0%	6.0%
Outside Park	94.4%	5.6%
TOTAL	87.7%	12.3%

To place the provision of public housing in the Lake District into
perspective, it is useful to compare the areas of housing stress
inside and outside the Park using the County Council's criteria. An
area of housing stress was one with high overcrowding, unemployment
and sickness and where many houses lacked essential facilities such
as a W.C. Figure 14 shows that none of the areas of major housing
stress are in the Park's towns and only three rural parishes exhibit
stress. Initially this would suggest that the overall provision of
public housing is adequate. However this view must be tempered by
studying the changes to the waiting list of applicants for a council
house.

The waiting list helps measure the need for housing and changes in
the waiting list measure how successfully the local authority is
meeting that need. An analysis was made of the applicants removed
from the Allerdale waiting list between 31st March 1979 and 31st
March 1980 to see how many had obtained a council house. The
argument here is that providing the right number of council houses to
meet a given need is only half the exercise. The other half is to
provide the houses quickly enough. If there is too long a delay,
then some applicants will not be able or willing to wait and they will
seek some other solution and this could involve migration out of the
Lake District. Delay in providing housing could act as a rationing
device in the sense that there are more people wanting a council
house than can be accommodated immediately (hence the waiting list)
and the scarce commodity of housing is partly allocated by people's
differing ability to wait for a house. This ability to wait need not
necessarily have any simple or direct relationship with the need for
housing as measured by housing points.

The waiting list in Allerdale District grew by 72 households
between March 1979 and March 1980. This was the net result of about
125 households joining the list and 53 households leaving it. The
53 households are the equivalent of 13.3 per cent of the households

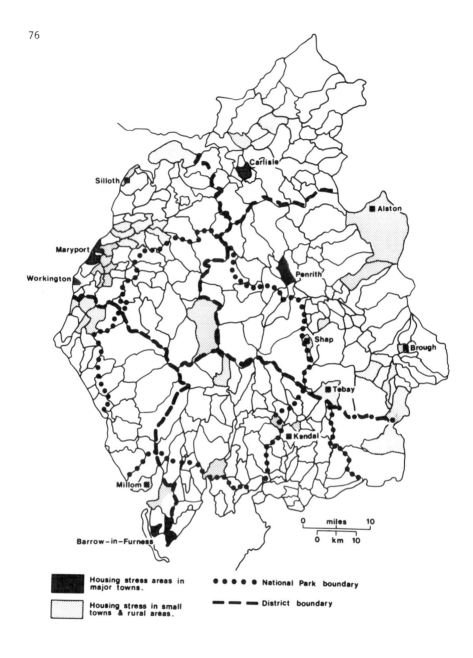

FIG.14.   Housing stress in Cumbria (after C.C.C. and L.D.S.P.B.,
           1976).

TABLE 12. Status and current housing of households leaving Allerdale
waiting list, March 1979 to March 1980

	Owner-occupier	Tenant	Lodger	TOTAL
Single	0%	1.9%	9.4%	11.3%
Family	3.8%	18.9%	15.1%	37.7%
O.A.P.	18.9%	18.9%	13.2%	50.9%
TOTAL	22.6%	39.6%	37.7%	99.9% = 53 households

TABLE 13. Reasons for leaving waiting list for council house in
Allerdale.

Reason	Number of Households
Rehoused by Allerdale D.C. in first choice parish	13
Rehoused by Allerdale D.C. in other parish	4
Rehoused by another District Council	1
Rehoused by Housing Association	1
Found own accommodation	4
Requested removal from list	7
Left Allerdale	6
No longer at last address	12
Rehoused in old folks' home	1
Applicant deceased	4
TOTAL	53 households

on the waiting list in March 1979 or 15.7 per cent of the households on the list in March 1979 and resident in the Park.

If the status (single, family etc.) and current housing of the 53 households which left the list (Table 12) is compared with the status and housing of those still on it in March 1980, it is apparent that those leaving the list were drawn disproportionately from the lodgers and those living in, irrespective of whether they were single, families or pensioners. Tenants who were pensioners also left the list in larger numbers than expected while owner-occupiers of whatever status left the list less than expected. Those leaving the list showed the same bias towards coming from Keswick and wishing a house there as was seen on the full Allerdale list although neither bias was quite so extreme. The reasons why these 53 households were removed from the waiting list are recorded in Table 13.

Only 32.1 per cent left the list because Allerdale District Council gave them a house. Others found their own accommodation and some died. Many had left their last known address and had not replied to a district council circular enquiring whether they wished their application renewed. It is not known whether these people had found other housing in Allerdale or had left the district completely. Further study showed that families and pensioners had been more successful in securing a council house than had single people, while families also figured prominently among those who had left the area and whose address was not known. Similarly tenants had been housed faster than owner-occupiers or lodgers both of whom had often moved away.

It is clear from Table 14 that the district council has spread its efforts across the scale of need as measured by the points score. Three-quarters of those whose addresses were not known had fewer than 21 points and several had not yet been allocated points.

It is also clear that those leaving the list for whatever reason, have a fairly similar distribution of housing points to those remaining on the lists. This suggests that although allocation of a council house does much to reduce the list at the needier end, other processes such as personal initiative and migration reduce the list among those of low and moderate need. It is also possible to look at the period of time people have spent on the list before leaving it for their various reasons and Table 15 provides a cross-tabulation of those leaving the list and their length of time on the list.

Those who had left their last address or found their own accommodation tended to have been on the waiting list for only a short period. Those who had left Allerdale had mostly been on the list for 1 to 3 years while those obtaining a council house were spread over the recent and long-term applicants. Some obtained a house very quickly - accepting a house in another parish seemed to help even if the household's points score was on the low side. Many spent 2 or 3 years before getting a house while a few spent over 4 years waiting.

TABLE 14. Households' reasons for leaving waiting list and their housing points

Reason	None Awarded	1-5	6-10	11-15	16-20	21-25	>25
				Points Score			
Rehoused by Allerdale D.C. in 1st choice parish					5	6	2
Rehoused by Allerdale D.C. in other parish			1	2	1		
Rehoused by other District Council	1						
Rehoused by Housing Association				1			
Found own accommodation	1			1		2	
Requested removal from list	1				3	3	
Left Allerdale	2				3	1	
No longer at last address	4			4	2	2	
Rehoused in old folks' home				1			
Applicant deceased	1				1	2	
TOTAL	10	0	1	9	15	16	2
TOTAL as % of those with points		0	2.3	20.9	34.9	37.2	4.7
Full Allerdale residents list, March 1980		0	1.8	14.9	45.1	33.8	4.4

TABLE 15. Households' reasons for leaving waiting list and their period on waiting list.

Reason	Period on waiting list before leaving it				
	0-1yr	1.1yr-2yrs	2.1yr-3yrs	3.1yr-4yrs	>4 yrs
Rehoused by Allerdale D.C. in 1st choice parish	4	1	5	1	2
Rehoused by Allerdale D.C. in other parish	2	1	0	0	1
Rehoused by other District Council	1	0	0	0	0
Rehoused by Housing Association	1	0	0	0	0
Found own accommodation	3	0	1	0	0
Requested removal from list	2	2	3	0	0
Left Allerdale	1	2	2	1	0
No longer at last address	6	4	2	0	0
Rehoused in old folks' home	1	0	0	0	0
Applicant deceased	0	1	1	1	1
TOTAL	21	11	14	3	4

To explain why some applicants left the list quickly and some
remained on it for a long time, an analysis was made of the points
scores of those obtaining a council house quickly and those
obtaining one only after many years. One would expect that rapid
allocation would be due to having a high points score and long
delayed allocation due to a low points score. However Table 16 shows
this is not the case.

Some people with few points obtained a house in under a year while
some with over 25 points had to wait over 2 years. Although there
are only 17 cases in the study period, housing points are not a good
predictor of the time needed to obtain a council house and discussion
with Allerdale District Housing Department confirmed that they use
the points system as only one indicator of need. Less easily
quantifiable information on the person's exact situation, the
urgency for re-housing and the benefits to the local authority from
re-housing particular individuals are also used to determine
allocation. This observation may help to temper the sometimes
excessive weight given to points systems as the key to council house
allocation. Such systems may be more important in urban areas where
the number of applicants and houses is so much greater than in rural
areas. In the countryside the system may well be more flexible, less
predictable and more humane, relying on broader criteria of merit for
providing housing.

The low proportion of people who believed themselves in need of a
council house and who were re-housed by the council is rather
perturbing. Rapid rehousing by the council may only be possible
because two-thirds of applicants find their own houses, die or
migrate from the Lake District. The question of which of those who
cannot buy a house shall be allocated a council house seems relevant
in this context. The relationship between the number of council
houses, their speed of allocation to applicants and depopulation of
the low incomes group from the countryside clearly needs some
investigation. The proposed sale of council houses to sitting
tenants and therefore, one assumes, the shrinkage of the council-
house sector in the short term makes such further study increasingly
important.

4.5 PRIVATE HOUSING IN THE LAKE DISTRICT

The two major planning matters relating to public housing in the
Lake District have concerned the location of public housing and the
number built. In the private sector, the principal planning problem
in the 1950s was the fear that too few houses were being built while
by the 1970s it was a fear of too many being built. In the 1980s it
is arguable that the problem will be the relationship between public
and private housing. To explore this in more detail it is first
necessary to examine the relationship between planning and the
private housing sector.

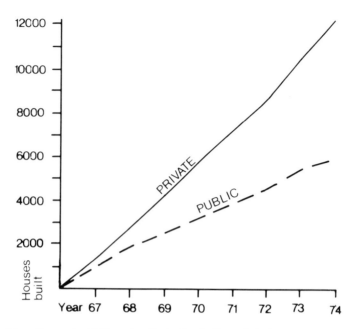

FIG. 15.   House building in Cumbria (after C.C.C. and L.D.S.P.B., 1976).

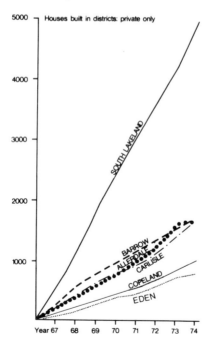

FIG.16.   Private house building by district, 1967-74 (after C.C.C.
and L.D.S.P.B., 1976).

TABLE 16. Length of time on waiting list and points score

Period on List	Points Score						
	0-5	6-10	11-15	16-20	21-25	Over 25	TOTAL
0 - 1 year	0	1	1	2	2	0	6
1. 1 - 2 years	0	0	0	2	0	0	2
2. 1 - 3 years	0	0	0	1	2	2	5
3. 1 - 4 years	0	0	0	0	1	0	1
Over 4 years	0	0	1	1	1	0	3
TOTAL	0	1	2	6	6	2	17

4.5.1 EARLY HOUSING POLICY

Prior to 1974 housing policy was unashamedly expansionist. The Development Plan for the National Park, which was drawn up in 1956 and reviewed in 1965, allowed a considerable number of new houses to be built including some quite large estates. The location of the new houses was carefully controlled so that estates were only built in the larger settlements like Windermere, while smaller-scale developments were permitted in villages and even hamlets. The result was a 45 per cent increase in the number of houses in the Park between 1951 and 1976, with the private sector by far the more dynamic, particularly in South Lakeland as Figures 15 and 16 show.

This new public and private construction and the availability of improvement grants greatly improved the physical quality of houses in the Lake District. Although only Cumbria (Figure 17) and district data are available (Table 17), there is no reason to suppose that the National Park has not shared in the general improvement, even given that the definition of an adequate house has been raised over the last twenty years. In 1961 for example an outside W.C. was considered adequate while by 1971 only an inside W.C. was deemed adequate.

The Lake District Planning Board allowed so many new houses to be built because, although they might be quite expensive and hence the proportion occupied by people employed locally quite small, nevertheless the more private houses that were built, the more likely it was that local people would obtain one. It might be necessary to build several times as many houses as local need required in order to meet that demand, but the Planning Board felt this was a price worth paying to provide housing for local workers. Some would occupy the new houses and others would move into the houses vacated by those who bought the new houses. It was a policy which assumed a filtering process could take place since it was hoped that the new private houses were adding to the supply of houses faster than the growth of external demand for Lakeland houses.

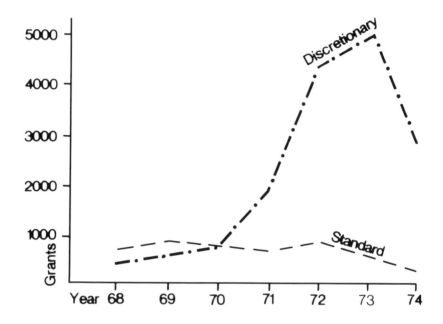

FIG.17. Improvement grants in Cumbria, 1968-74 (after C.C.C. and
L.D.S.P.B., 1976).

TABLE 17. Households lacking one or more standard household
    amenities.*

District	1951	1961	1971
Carlisle	11,697 (43%)	6,832 (22%)	6,557 (19.5%)
Allerdale	13,823 (52%)	8,794 (30%)	5,908 (19%)
Eden	6,889 (56%)	3,787 (30%)	1,933 (14.2%)
Copeland	9,172 (50%)	5,677 (27%)	3,429 (15.3%)
South Lakeland	Not available	4,948 (20%)	3,376 (10.9%)
Barrow	Not available	6,446 (27%)	4,795 (18.7%)
Cumbria	Not available	36,484 (26%)	26,021 (16.5%)
Cumberland and Westmorland	47,382 (48%)		

* A stove or cooker (1951 only)

  A fixed bath or shower

  A hot water supply (except in 1951)

  A water closet inside home (except in 1951 and 1961)

Source: Cumbria C.C. (1976) p.122.

A high rate of house building was seen as a prerequisite for
preventing rural depopulation and the cumulative social and economic
malaise which this caused. The rural areas of the Park lost 6.8 per
cent of their population between 1951 and 1971 (Lake District S.P.B.,
1978 p.150). In fact, the Park's population was roughly static
between 1951 and 1971. However this concealed the strong growth in
towns such as Windermere where 1500 houses were built after 1955 and
the population rose by 35 per cent in the twenty years to 1971.
Conversely there was continuing depopulation in 61 of the Park's 82
parishes (Figure 18). In the former counties of Cumberland and
Westmorland, 25 of the 67 parishes in the Park had over 30 per cent
fewer 15 to 25 year olds in 1971 than there were 5 to 14 year olds
ten years earlier (Figure 19). The corollary was that in 1971 the
proportion of the Park's population who were retired was already 6
percentage points higher than the England and Wales average of 16
per cent.

The central planning task was identified as stemming a rural
depopulation which had been continuing for a century with the
attendant loss of a local labour force. Socially balanced
communities with local, year-round employment should be preserved in
the face of the perennial loss of jobs from agriculture and quarrying.
These shed 32 per cent and 52 per cent respectively of their employees
in the sixties while employment in woodworking industries and on the

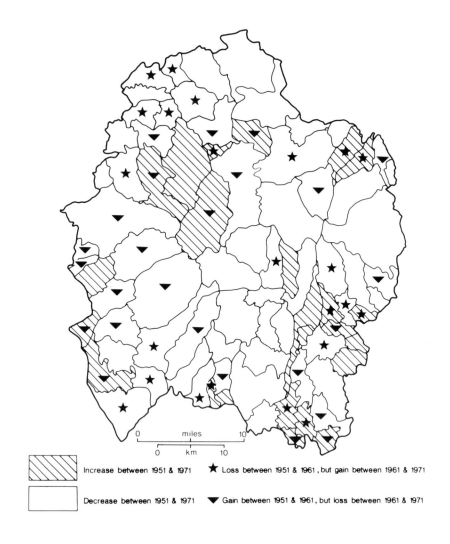

FIG.18.   Population change by parish, 1951-71 (after L.D.S.P.B.,
                1978).

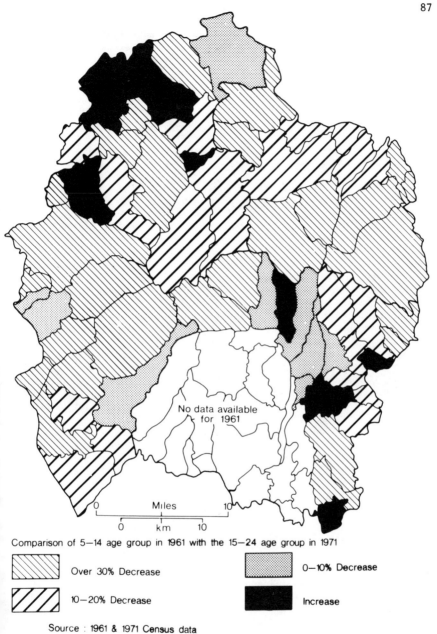

Comparison of 5—14 age group in 1961 with the 15—24 age group in 1971

	Over 30% Decrease		0—10% Decrease
	10—20% Decrease		Increase

Source : 1961 & 1971 Census data

FIG.19.   Population structure by parish, 1961-71 (after L.D.S.P.B.,
          1978).

railways had also declined (Cumbria C.C. and Lake District S.P.B., 1976 p.73). Although Capstick's work (1972) had shown that depopulation was more often prompted by adverse employment prospects rather than a shortage of suitable housing, it was feared that industrial promotion would be stifled if houses were not available locally for employees. The only way of securing accommodation in the face of high house prices and external demand was to allocate much more land for housing and permit many houses to be built. With a plentiful supply of houses, their high price might even be reduced and there would be sufficient houses for local people, second-home owners and people retiring to the Lake District.

By the early 1970s, however, disquiet developed over the effects of this policy and centred on three main aspects. First, house prices remained high relative to those elsewhere in the region. Bennett reported in 1976 that two-bedroomed houses in the Park fetched between £2,000 and £6,000 more than such houses outside the Park (Bennett, 1976 pp. 24-5). Shucksmith conducted a fuller survey of house prices in the south-east Lake District and compared these with Northern Region figures (Shucksmith, 1980 p.10). He found that on average houses in the south-east of the Park were never less than fifty per cent more expensive than houses in the Northern Region and during periods of rapid inflation of house prices the differential rose to over one hundred per cent. These figures could however be exaggerated by the use of asking prices for houses in one local newspaper in the most popular district of the Park.

Second, concern was expressed at the high proportion of new houses which were bought by the retired or as second homes. In 1976 Bennett noted that nearly eleven per cent of all houses in the Park were second homes while by 1980 studies showed that this was either an under-estimate or the proportion had increased since then (Bennett, 1976 p.10 and Clark, forthcoming). In a survey of 344 houses and flats built since 1970 on estates of various sizes throughout the Park, the Special Planning Board found that 26 per cent were occupied as holiday or second homes and 40 per cent by retired people. These groups also accounted for 66 per cent of the occupants of nineteenth-century terraced housing which was surveyed at the same time.

Finally, the scale of building resulting from the policy was causing disquiet because of its effect on the landscape. In 1951 Bowness and Windermere were physically separate settlements but by 1970 new building had linked them into a virtually continuous built-up area. Similarly, there was disquiet that in some villages the rate of private building was altering the village's social and visual character. The village of Braithwaite is a good example of the scale of new building although it may be exceptional because of its proximity to Keswick and the upgraded A66 road between West Cumbria and the M6 motorway at Penrith (Figure 20). The demand from outsiders for houses was nowhere near being saturated and it persisted after 1974 when improvement grants and mortgage interest relief were abolished for second homes. While it is arguable that

89

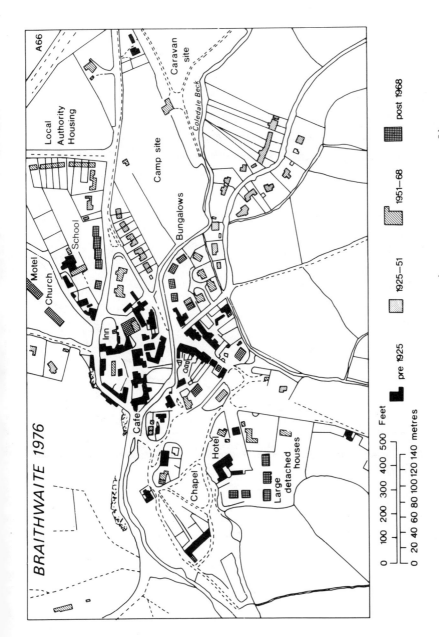

FIG.20.   The expansion of Braithwaite village, Cumbria (after L.D.S.P.B., 1978).

90

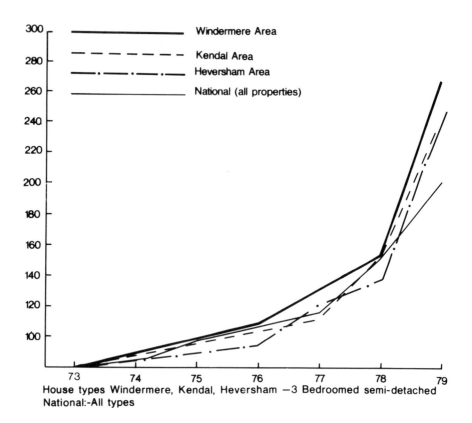

House types Windermere, Kendal, Heversham —3 Bedroomed semi-detached
National:-All types

FIG.21.   House prices in South Lakeland District (after L.D.S.P.B.,
           1980).

these subsidies had previously been capitalised into higher prices
for second homes, their removal had little detectable effect on
cheapening house prices in the Lake District relative to those elsewhere, as was shown by Shucksmith's evidence. Work by the Special
Planning Board showed that, by and large, the rate of increase in
house prices since 1973 had been comparable in Windermere which is
inside the Park and in the Kendal-Heversham area which is outside the
Park (Figure 21).

The high house prices are illustrated by advertisements selected
from a single issue of the Westmorland Gazette (Figure 22).
Properties with potential for hotels and bed and breakfast accommodation are highly priced, while holiday cottages like those
advertised in the Cumbria magazine represent a further drain on the
stock of houses available for permanent residents. The filtering of
houses down into the reach of the less well-off will only occur if
the price gap between the newer and the older houses is not too wide.
Clearly, existing houses have reached such a price that, even when
divided into flats, they are too expensive for most locally employed
people and are meeting a demand from outside Lakeland.

Finally, it was argued that there was insufficient land in the Park
to support a high rate of building. 'Most places have reached their
limit of development and, if substantial damage to the landscape is
to be avoided, future rates of building must be severely curtailed'
(C.C.C. and L.D.S.P.B., 1980, p.54). Implicitly, a different
aesthetic judgement on housing in the landscape could yield more
building land.

4.5.2 THE CHANGE OF POLICY

Disquiet over housing policy was initially articulated in
submissions to the Planning Board by organisations such as Young
Farmers Clubs and Women's Institutes which did small surveys of the
number of second homes and suggested that they should be discouraged
by, for example, a higher assessment for rating. Second homes were
popularly believed to inflate house prices and deprive young families
who wished to work locally of a house. In 1974 the Board held a
series of meetings with the public and district councils and were
again made aware of the extent of concern over the nexus of second
homes, house prices and the out-migration of local people unable to
obtain a house. In 1976, statistical evidence on the extent of
second homes in the Lake District National Park became available for
the first time with the publication of Bennett's survey which had
been commissioned by the Special Planning Board. Although the definition of 'second home' used here is open to discussion, the survey
showed that in some parishes the proportion of second homes exceeded
30 per cent and averaged 11 per cent in the whole of the National
Park (Figure 23). At the same time the Special Planning Board held
public meetings on the National Park Plan and housing emerged as
second to traffic as the greatest source of concern. Over 540 people
submitted written comments on the plan and 90 per cent of them wanted
some restriction on the ownership of houses by outsiders.

FIGURE 22. Some advertisements for houses, cottages and flats in Cumbria, 1981.

From: The Westmorland Gazette, May 29th, 1981 - p.27.

AMBLESIDE   £48,500

Elevated position. New detached Bungalow due for completion in June. Panoramic views. Full gas central heating, double Garage. Well planned and appointed. Spacious L-shaped Lounge/Dining Room, Kitchen, three Bedrooms, Bathroom, separate W.C.

AMBLESIDE   £39,500

New semi-detached Bungalows. Outstanding panoramic views from elevated site in course of erection. First Bungalow ready July. Fully gas central heating. Lounge, Kitchen, two Bedrooms, Bathroom, double Garage.

STOCK PARK, NEWBY BRIDGE   From £30,000

Choice of five luxury one and two bedroom fully furnished apartments in converted Mansion, superb 120 acre parkland setting with mile of Lake frontage, boat park and launching facilities. Ideal holiday homes or investment - full letting service available.

CONISTON   £37,500

Detached Bungalow on south side of Coniston with views of Wetherlam. Convenient position for Coniston village, lake and the rest of the National Park. Porch, Hall, Lounge/Dining Room, Kitchen, two Bedrooms, Bathroom with full suite, enclosed Porch with Store and Fuel Store off. Gardens, parking space, possible Garage room.

OUTSKIRTS OF BOWNESS   £34,500

Holiday Flats. A Former Hotel is being converted into superb 1- and 2-bedroom Flats. Outstanding views of the fells, mountains and Lake. Individually serviced and private parking. Convenient for Marina, Golf Club and easy access to M6 spur. Only one available at the moment.

BETWEEN BOWNESS AND NEWBY BRIDGE   Offers around £35 000

A most attractive Traditional Lakeland Cottage. Small Garden. Large Garage. Ideal as a weekend holiday home.

GRASMERE   £50,000

A Property with excellent Lakeland views being the centre portion of a former detached residence convenient for the village yet set off the main road at the approach to Helvellyn. The property is in need of some modernisation and the accommodation provides Entrance Porch, Vestibule, Hall, Lounge, Kitchen, Pantry,

FIGURE 22 (Continued)

GRASMERE (Continued)   £50,000

3 Bedrooms and Bathroom. Easily maintained level Garden. Garage.

WINDERMERE PARK   £57,000

Modern Detached Bungalow in good order throughout with beautiful
Gardens and fine views of the fells and mountains. Lounge,
Fitted Kitchen, 3 Good Bedrooms all with fitted wardrobes,
Bathroom with W.C., separate W.C., Large Double Garage. Gas
central heating.

From: Cumbria - Lake District Life 30(10) 1981 p.598

CUMBRIA - Fringe of Lake District. Holiday houses, sleeps 2/6.
Storage heaters. Clean, comfortable. £30.00 /£65.00
_____Farm, Sebergham, Carlisle, Cumbria.

CUMBRIA - Penrith, Ullswater 6 miles. Spacious self-catering
accommodation. S/C. Sleeps 2-10, Col. T.V., C.H. Fully equipped.

DERWENTWATER - Holiday Cottage, modern facilities, magnificent
views, own grounds, private access onto "Catbells", no young
children. Gun dogs welcome. Low season £40 to High season
£120 VAT included. Sleeps 5.

EDEN VALLEY - Carefully restored 18th century stone cottage in
small village. Sleeps 5. Garden. TV. All mod. cons. Details:
Thornhill Terrace, Sunderland.

FURNISHED COTTAGE - 4 bedrooms. Hartsop, Patterdale.

GRANGE-OVER-SANDS AREA AND LAKELAND COAST.

Furnished holiday accommodation. We have a wide selection of
Cottages, Bungalows, Maisonettes and Flats. Apply (stating
number in party and dates required) to Messrs. _____,
Estate Agents, Grange-over-Sands.

KESWICK - 2 miles S.C. holiday flat. Sleeps 2/4. Braithwaite.

KESWICK - A charming cottage, sleeps 5, modern fitted kitchen,
colour TV, no pets.

KESWICK - Comfortable holiday flats. All electric, country
setting. Stamp please. _____ Grange, Keswick,
Cumbria.

KESWICK, Cumbria - Modern two-bedroomed bungalow. Central
Heating. Sleeps 5/7, plus cot. Yorks.

94

FIGURE 22 (Continued)

KESWICK - Exclusive holiday flats on hill farm with
commanding views. Open all year.

LAKE DISTRICT - Foot of Kentmere Valley. Holiday bungalow
sleeps 7.

LAKE DISTRICT, near Haweswater/Ullswater - Comfortable
furnished holiday cottage, sleeps 6. Available throughout
the year.

LAKE DISTRICT - 4 miles Keswick. Ground floor modern s.c.
flat. Sleeps 5, plus cot. Television. No meters. Apply
Burlington Road, Blackpool.

LAKE DISTRICT, Lower Ennerdale. Delightful, 2 bedroomed
holiday flat, sleeps 5. Self-contained. Open all year.

LAKE DISTRICT - S.C. cottage in Broughton-in-Furness.
Sleeps 6. S.a.e.

LAKELAND - Cottage at Gosforth sleeps 4/6. Good base for
family holidays. Sea, Lakes and beautiful scenery.

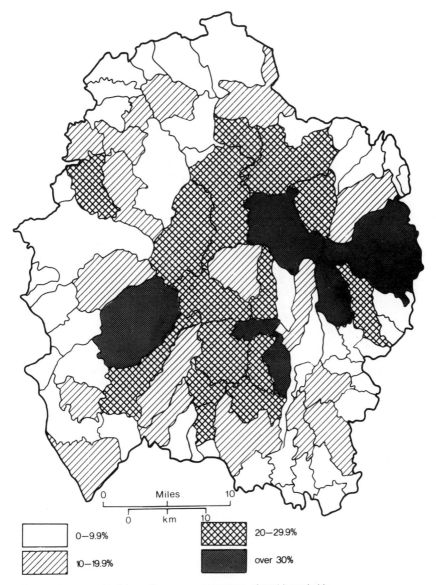

Second homes and holiday cottages as a percentage of total households

0–9.9%	20–29.9%
10–19.9%	over 30%

FIG.23.   Second homes by parish in the Lake District National
           Park (after Bennett, 1976).

The Board not only received expressions of concern at local level, they also received revised national guidelines on what should be the attitude to development in national parks. This was contained in the Sandford Report (1974) and was given official sanction by Circular 4/76 from the Department of the Environment in 1976. In broad terms the Sandford Report concluded that where there was a conflict in a national park between development and the protection of the character of the landscape, the presumption should be that the needs of the landscape would determine policy. The emphasis in policy should be shifted in favour of the park authorities' statutory duty to preserve landscape and prevent developments which would alter the landscape and this new emphasis should also apply to housing policy.

As a result, the members of the Board held a number of informal seminars and concluded that they needed to do something to help local people obtain housing and to preserve more rigorously the Lakeland landscape. Quite what they should do was not apparent since the obvious solution of building more council houses was not an option they could pursue since they were solely a planning authority, without any control over the four district councils which provided council housing in the National Park. They characterised their options as either continuing the policy of granting many planning permissions or restricting development. The Planning Board's officers were instructed to find a way of achieving such restriction. Their first response was to suggest the widespread use of local person conditions on planning permissions, but the officers felt this would be unworkable in practice and they were instructed to find another method.

The second proposal, which was accepted, was a two-pronged policy. First, the rate of housing development was to be severely restricted so as to preserve the landscape and character of the Park. Only 70 houses a year would be built which was the minimum needed for local employment, reduced household size and demolition. Second, the small number of houses which were built would be reserved exclusively for local people using powers vested in all planning authorities under Section 52 of the Town and Country Planning Act of 1971.

'52(1) A local planning authority may enter into an agreement with any person interested in land in their area for the purpose of restricting or regulating the development or use of land either permanently, or during such period as may be prescribed by the agreement; and any such agreement may contain such incidental and consequential provisions (...) as appear to the local planning authority to be necessary or expedient (...)'

Previously these powers, and similar ones in the 1947 Planning Act had been used to allow houses to be built in open country for agricultural and similar workers despite the general presumption against such development (Town and Country Planning Act 1971). In the National Park approval would be given for a new house only if the occupier would live there for over six months of each year and was a

person 'employed or to be employed or last employed locally and the
dependents of such a person living with him or her and the widow or
widower or such a person'. This agreement would act as a restrictive
covenant on the house which would be registered as a local land
charge and as such would be binding on all subsequent owners of the
house. This presented the prospect of creating a sub-market of
houses exclusively occupied by locally employed, full-time residents
and protected from purchase by outsiders as has happened in some of
the Channel Islands. Since the demand from potential second-home
owners would be excluded, these houses ought to be cheaper than
comparable property open to all bidders. In this way positive
discrimination in favour of local workers would be applied as a
counterweight to the inflationary policy of severely restricting the
number of new houses. The Section 52 policy would mitigate the
harsher effects on the local population of the reduction on aesthetic
grounds in new house building.

That this policy of increased intervention in the free market of
private housing was accepted by the Special Planning Board is perhaps
as remarkable as the policy itself, given the composition of the
Board. In 1974, the reorganisation of local government in England
and Wales had amalgamated Cumberland, Westmorland and the Furness
District of Lancashire into the new county of Cumbria. For the first
time, the area of the Lake District National Park was included within
only one county and the Planning Board was re-constituted as the
Special Planning Board. In 1977 a new group of Board members was
appointed by Cumbria County Council, most of them Conservatives, yet
after discussions and site visits, fifteen of the Board's members
agreed to the policy with nine opposed. The simple desire to help
local people and protect the character of the Lakes had prevailed
over regional and political affiliations to produce an approval of
one of the most radical attempts in Great Britain to intervene in a
rural housing market.

Although the policy was included in both the National Park Plan and
in the Joint Structure Plan with Cumbria County Council, there were
three areas of concern felt by Board members over the policy. The
first concerned the practicality of enforcement. The Board received
advice from counsel that the policy was legal but the sanctions
which might be applied if a Section 52 agreement was broken were not
clear. The second concern was over the definition of "local". If
only local people can acquire new private houses, there must be a
definition of local which is neither so restrictive that re-sale of
the house is impossible nor so wide as to allow in commuters, for
example, to Manchester. The third concern was over the effect the
policy would have on house prices. An inflationary effect on the
price of existing houses was anticipated since the demand for second
homes would be deflected from new houses to the existing stock of
houses which was not affected by the policy. However this was seen
as the inevitable quid pro quo for achieving the broader objective of
landscape protection and aiding local people. It was hoped initially
that the new Section 52 houses for local people would be cheaper and
so some benefit would accrue to the marginal house buyer. Despite

these areas of uncertainty, the policy was approved. No alternative methods of achieving the same objective were discussed nor were the effects on the parts of Cumbria outside the Park considered. The policy was the Special Planning Board's own and as such is a measure of their autonomy from Cumbria County Council on planning matters.

4.5.3 ASSESSING THE NEW POLICY

So far, the two policies of reducing the rate of house building and ensuring local occupancy have been presented separately for convenience of description. In reality they are inseparably linked. The operation of the local occupancy policy will deter builders from applying for planning permission which in turn will aid the policy of reducing the rate of house building. Conversely, the reduction in house building could raise the price of existing houses so much that the case for something like the local occupancy policy is strength- ened. They form a two-pronged housing policy and have to be assessed together.

The assessment of a long-term policy which operates at the margin of the housing stock and which has only been in operation for three years cannot be comprehensive but some guidance can be obtained from studies conducted in 1980. The policy is likely to offer distinctive costs and benefits to different groups in the Park and these are set out below. Initially it is assumed that the policy succeeds as was intended in creating a sub-market of cheaper houses for local people and that it raises further the price of existing houses, due to deflected demand and the restriction of the supply of new houses. It is envisaged that the existing stock of houses will still contribute some 90 per cent of the stock in 1991. These assumptions will be examined later.

For existing house owners, the principal advantages will be a greater capital gain on the sale of their present house as the demand for second homes is deflected to the existing stock of houses which are not covered by Section 52 agreements. This would be offset if they wished to buy another house in the Park. On balance many of this group or their heirs will gain from the policy. Capital gains may also be experienced by house owners outside the Park if some of the demand for second homes is deflected to other parts of Cumbria.

For new non-local house owners, the principal disadvantage will be the higher cost of the existing stock of houses which could reduce the number of such people and make them more socially and financially exclusive. The higher price of houses for this group could be partially offset by higher tax relief on mortgages for people on higher marginal tax rates. On balance this group should lose financially from the policy.

The critical group, however, are the new local owners of Section 52 houses. For this group the principal advantage will be that Section 52 houses will be cheaper, while selling an existing house in the

Park to buy a comparable Section 52 will lead to a windfall capital gain. However, many Section 52 houses are likely to be 'one-off' commissions - on average, only seventy a year are envisaged up to 1991 - and so they could be more expensive than comparable property on a housing estate. The greatest saving will accrue to the new local house owner who already owns the plot of land for the house. The new local house owner is therefore unlikely <u>a priori</u> to be the marginal house buyer. The disadvantages for this group are that, firstly, it may take longer to sell a Section 52 house since the buyer must also meet the Section 52 conditions. This in turn may have financial consequences (e.g. a bridging loan) and may affect mobility of employment. The financial benefit of a cheaper house could also be offset if building societies lend less on these houses. In addition, trading up from a small Section 52 house to a larger free market house could involve an unusually large financial step. Finally, the amount of capital gain from the sale of a Section 52 house may be less than normal. The balance of advantage for this group - one of the critical groups for the policy - is difficult to predict since it will depend largely on personal circumstances.

The occupants of privately rented and council housing may find that the easier transition of the preceding group into the private sector will reduce pressure on rented housing and allow a filtering process. However, this will only happen if the Section 52 house owners would have looked to the rented sectors in the absence of this policy. The advantage to those entering the privately rented sector could be eroded if the greater cost of second homes led to an unsatisfied demand for them being deflected into an increasing number of holiday lets which would compete with renting to local people. Similarly if the greater cost of second homes in the Park deflects demand to the many attractive areas of Cumbria outside the Park, then the privately rented sector could be under greater pressure in these areas as well. The council house tenants - who comprise only 13 per cent of house-holds in the Park - will be better served buying their council house at a discount under the Housing Act, 1980 rather than trying to buy a Section 52 house.

As will be seen later, it is still premature to quantify these costs and benefits and to assess the validity of the assumptions from which they are derived, but one can move towards this by examining five critical areas.

<u>Number of houses built.</u>

Between September 1977 and August 1980, 104 Section 52 agreements were concluded covering 173 houses and in August 1980 another 23 agreements were under discussion. The completed agreements are shown in Figure 24. Only 13 houses had been built by August 1980 (Figure 25), 45 were under construction and 19 had obtained approval of building regulations although construction had not yet started. Table 18 shows that the Section 52 houses had advanced towards completion no slower than those houses approved without Section 52

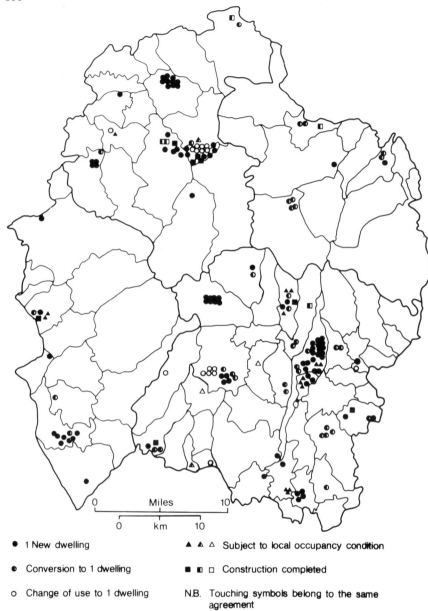

- ● 1 New dwelling
- ◖ Conversion to 1 dwelling
- ○ Change of use to 1 dwelling

- ▲ ▲ △ Subject to local occupancy condition
- ■ ◪ □ Construction completed
- N.B. Touching symbols belong to the same agreement

FIG.24.   Distribution of completed Section 52 agreements.

TABLE 18. Status at February 1980 of houses approved between September 1977 and June 1979*

Status	Houses with S52 agreement	Houses without S52 agreement
Constructed	8.5%	5.5%
Started	25.4%	18.9%
Building regulations approved	3.4%	9.8%
Building regulations not approved	62.7%	65.8%
	100.0%	100.0%
	59 houses	164 houses

NOTE *Excludes Allerdale District

TABLE 19. Comparative house prices.

House type	No. of comparisons	Park Price	Average differential*	Park price as % of price outside park
4 bedroomed, detached	1	£48,500	£19,650	168%
3 bedroomed, detached bungalow	3	£31,750	£4,617	117%
2 bedroomed, not detached	4	£21,350	£2,588	114%
3 bedroomed, not detached	4	£23,950	£2,575	112%
	12			

*In all cases the Park price was higher than the price outside the Park by the average differential shown in this column.

102

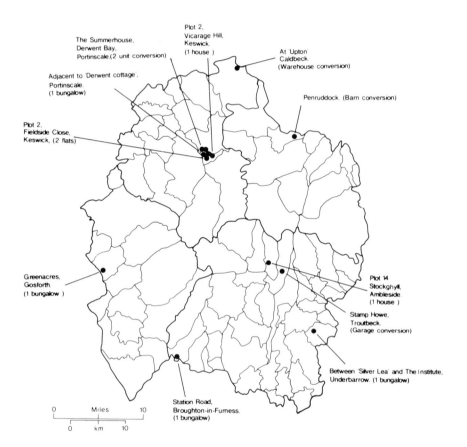

Plot 2,
Vicarage Hill,
Keswick.
(1 house)

The Summerhouse,
Derwent Bay,
Portinscale.(2 unit conversion)

At 'Upton'
Caldbeck.
(Warehouse conversion)

Adjacent to 'Derwent cottage',
Portinscale.
(1 bungalow)

Penruddock. (Barn conversion)

Plot 2,
Fieldside Close,
Keswick, (2 flats)

Greenacres,
Gosforth.
(1 bungalow)

Plot 14
Stockghyll,
Ambleside.
(1 house)

Stamp Howe,
Troutbeck.
(Garage conversion)

Between 'Silver Lea' and The Institute,
Underbarrow. (1 bungalow)

Station Road,
Broughton-in-Furness.
(1 bungalow)

0   Miles   10

0   km   10

FIG.25.   Completed Section 52 houses, August 1980.

agreements in the same period.

There has been a good deal of initial scepticism about the policy particularly among local lawyers and estate agents. A survey of the twenty people who had obtained permission for a house with a Section 52 agreement before June 1979 but who had not started construction in March 1980 showed a wide range of reasons for the delay among the twelve replies received. Most related to a change of job or detailed site problems such as poor drainage. Principally however they were waiting to see if the policy would be declared illegal through a test case. If, on the contrary, the policy is declared legal and is included in the Joint Structure Plan for the Park which is currently under examination, then one might expect the rate of building to increase.

Price of Section 52 Houses

The belief that Section 52 houses will be cheaper stems from the argument that house prices in the Park are higher than those outside it wholly or in large part because of the inflationary effect of the demand from potential second-home owners and people retiring to the Park. There is no doubt that house prices in the Park are high. When property of similar size is compared in Windermere, which is in the Park, and the Kendal-Heversham area outside the Park, the former is clearly the more expensive. Another survey in 1980 compared the price of standard types of new houses built by the same builder and offered for sale simultaneously inside and outside the Park on estates of comparable size. The houses, being new, were sold at a fixed and well-advertised price by the builder or his agent, and because they were on sale simultaneously on estates of similar size, many sources of price variation concerned with construction, company efficiency and pricing policy were eliminated. Unlike many other methods of measuring spatial variations in house prices, this eliminates most sources of price changes except for location. Of course, there may still be differences of site or landscaping which are not controlled but the technique seems to bring one closer to perfect comparability than hitherto in house-price surveys.

Twelve such comparisons were made between the prices of comparable groups of property being sold in May 1980 by two building companies on estates of similar size inside and outside the National Park. Matters such as garage provision and central heating were standard-ised before the comparison of prices was made. Two estates in the Park and ten different estates outside it were used and the results are given in Table 19.

In 11 of the 12 estate-by-estate comparisons, the National Park house price was the higher. There is some tendency for the comparisons to be in the less popular western part of the Park and in the parts of Allerdale, Copeland and Eden districts outside the Park. It is arguable that house prices in absolute terms will be higher in the eastern part of the Park and in South Lakeland outside the Park, however the differential between the Park and outside should be the same.

The number of comparisons is, of course, small since the study was limited by the number of cases in May 1980 where a builder was selling similar housing both inside and outside the Park. However it appears that the price in the Park of new houses is between 10 per cent and 20 per cent higher than the price outside the Park at the lower end of the market. The differential may be substantially higher at the upper end of the market. However measuring price differentials at the top end of the market will always be difficult since there is less chance of comparable property appearing on the market simultaneously. Therefore, the differential for a four-bedroomed detached house in Table 19 is unreliable and should be treated with particular caution.

The differential in price may be due to higher construction costs because of longer travelling times into the Park for building workers and also to the Planning Board regulations on slate roofs which can add £2,000 to the price of a house. These extra costs would not be reduced by the new housing policy. Instead the envisaged restriction on the number of houses built may raise production costs, as the housing estates will be smaller and land prices per hectare are higher as smaller plots are brought. Alternatively, the differential may be due to higher profit margins for the builder, particularly at the top end of the market, in which case the policy should help reduce prices. So far it has not been possible to assess the actual resale price of the Section 52 houses which have already been built as none has yet been resold. If the greatest effect of the policy in reducing house prices proves to be for houses costing over £40,000, it is not clear how valuable is the claim that local need is being met. On the other hand, while the price of Section 52 houses may be higher than if they were on a large estate, they might have been higher still without the Section 52 policy, given the need to reduce the rate of house construction and the extreme scarcity value of a new house in the Lake District.

The Building Societies' Reaction

Evidence from the survey mentioned earlier of private individuals who had not yet built a Section 52 house despite getting planning permission, suggested that few were deterred from building because they could not get a mortgage. Only one of the twelve respondents mentioned this as a specific cause of delay. A survey of the eleven Section 52 houses occupied in July 1980 showed that four had been built with mortgages from four different building societies. A third survey conducted by the Special Planning Board examined building societies' general attitude to property with Section 52 agreements. This showed that most of those which replied were willing to lend on such property, two indicating that they would lend only seventy to eighty per cent of the free market valuation. If this were wide-spread, it could partially negate the benefit to local people of any reduction in house price caused by the policy. However neither

society had actually lent on such property. In one case a building
society declared itself totally opposed to any involvement with the
local occupancy policy, whereas in fact it had already given a
mortgage on a Section 52 house. Clearly the attitudes of the
building societies are still at a formative stage and they must be
monitored carefully since they will be crucial in determining the
scale of the financial effects on local home buyers from the policies.

Definition of 'local'

The word 'local' has to be defined with respect to the distance
between where a person lives - the Section 52 house - and where that
person works or, if retired, used to work. If the radius of
permitted commuting is too narrow, people could be prevented from
getting a job or changing jobs. Too wide a radius could leave the
policy open to abuse. Although the definition of 'local' is
considered separately in each case, the most common in the 104
agreements concluded so far is that 'local' means the area of the
District Council within which the house is situated (Table 20). This
definition is used in fifty-nine cases and in five others, where the
house was near the boundary of two Districts, the permitted area of
commuting was one District and a specified radius around the house.
In nineteen cases an area smaller than a District was specified -
usually certain named parishes - or only the part of the District
within the Park. These definitions allow commuting of up to about
thirty kilometres with either Windscale (the main source of new jobs
in Cumbria), Penrith, Ulverston or Kendal as possible places of
employment. This seems a not unreasonable definition under today's
conditions of personal mobility and declining employment in the
countryside.

The legality and enforcement of the policy

The policy's legality is not yet clear as there has been no
challenge to it in the courts. The Special Planning Board believe
that it is not ultra vires. It took eight years for the legality of
using Section 52 type of agreements to reserve new houses for
agricultural workers to be established, so there is time yet for a
legal challenge to emerge. Since July 1979 applicants who have
refused to sign an agreement have had their application approved
subject to a local person condition. This achieves the same effect
as an agreement but, because it has been imposed on the applicant, it
leaves him in a stronger position to appeal to the Secretary of State
against its imposition. In two cases an appeal has been made
although the results of the appeals are not yet known.

The enforceability of the policy is similarly unclear for want of
a test case. The sanctions in the event of an unremedied breach of
agreement would presumably be an injunction, damages or even
eviction. It is not clear whether the policy could withstand the
legal and political strains of such enforcement. The Special
Planning Board clearly hope that the policy will be accepted
voluntarily and they can point to the 104 agreements completed so far

TABLE 20. Definitions of 'local' in Section 52 agreements.

1. Completed agreements

	>1 D.C.	1 D.C.	1 D.C. within Park	>1 P.C.	1 D.C. or within radius specified	Local occup. condit.	Other	TOTAL
S. Lakeland	5	36	-	2	1	10	3	57
Allerdale	4	13	1	2	3	2	1	26
Copeland	4	6	-	1	1	1	1	14
Eden	1	4	2	-	-	-	-	7
TOTAL	14	59	3	5	5	13	5	104

2. Proceeding agreements

	>1 D.C.	1 D.C.	1 D.C. within Park	>1 P.C.	1 D.C. or within radius specified	Local occup. condit.	Other	TOTAL
S. Lakeland	-	13	-	-	-	1	-	14
Allerdale	-	2	-	1	-	2	1	6
Copeland	-	-	-	1	-	-	-	1
Eden	-	2	-	-	-	-	-	2
TOTAL	-	17	-	2	-	3	1	23

>1 D.C. = the area of more than one district council.
>1 P.C. = the area of more than one parish council.

where it has been. It appears that it may be possible to circumvent
the spirit of these agreements but so far the occupants of the
Section 52 houses are known to be abiding by the agreements.

4.5.4 IMPLICATIONS OF THE POLICY

The current policy for private housing reflects the sentiments of
many groups in the Lake District and of many members of the Special
Planning Board. It also represents a locally devised reaction to
the local manifestation of a widespread feature of housing in many
rural areas, namely an external demand for houses. The policy is
clearly playing its part in restricting the number of new houses and
ensuring that those which are built go to local people. The number of
houses for which planning permission has been granted has fallen
from 721 in 1972/73 to 143 in 1980/81 even though the total number of
planning applications has remained between 1000 and 1100 since 1974.
However it is not yet clear that it is the marginal house buyer who
will benefit and there is a suspicion that the policy may be
regressive. Certainly those who have built Section 52 houses so far
are individual families rather than the commercial builders who are
so strongly opposed to any restriction of house development in the
Park (National House Builders Federation, 1980). If the policy is
approved by central government, there will, in time, be a small sub-
market of houses which will be occupied by people rather better-off
than the marginal house buyer. The corollary is that there will be
additional capital gains for existing house owners if the demand for
second homes is deflected as predicted rather than stifled. This
represents a redistributive policy in favour of existing house owners
and those without a house but with the land for one. Consequently
in-migrants with local employment may derive less benefit than native
Lakelanders with a local job and some land. The benefits for the
new local house owners for whom the policy is partly tailored are
less predictable, being dependent on personal circumstances and the
attitudes of building societies towards the policy. Helping the
rather better-off house buyer may reduce the pressure on the council
sector but this is likely to be a relatively minor effect. The
waiting list of 1219 households in May 1980 for 2169 council houses
is unlikely to be shortened in any way by the policy. The reduction
of competition in the privately rented sector may be rather greater
unless the unsatisfied demand for second homes is transformed into a
higher demand for holiday lets. One is forced to question whether
meeting 'local need' is sufficiently important to warrant these
effects.

Had so indirect a planning mechanism to help local people obtain
housing been proposed ten years ago, it is unlikely that the policy
would have been adopted. In part, this would have been because the
climate of opinion both locally and nationally was not yet ready for
such a policy but, equally, there was then available the more direct
alternative of an enhanced programme of council house building and
the desire to preserve the landscape was not so strong. The option
of more council houses no longer exists to the same extent since the

funding for general purpose house building by district councils and
housing associations has been severely reduced and each of the four
Lakeland district councils faces greater demands for the reduced
programme of council house building from those areas outside the Park
such as Kendal, Penrith and West Cumbria. Equity-sharing and
partnership schemes between the four district councils and private
builders are also affected by the reduced circumstances of all
publicly funded housing authorities. Each of these options is being
tried or considered in the National Park but neither collectively nor
severally are they seen as capable of meeting all the local need in
the foreseeable future.

Despite all these uncertainties, there is no evident alternative
way under current planning legislation of helping less well-off local
people buy a house, once the decision has been taken on aesthetic
grounds to reduce the rate of private house building at a time when
fewer publicly financed houses will be built. The evolution of
national park policy into something distinctive, as befits
distinctive areas, has been called for by many commentators who have
seen the preservation of landscape as a statutory duty requiring
more support than it has been given previously. In this case,
however, landscape is being equated more with the socio-economic
character of the Lakes rather than its visual appearance and it is in
this sense that the Special Planning Board have been preserving the
landscape through housing policy. The question of whether they have
also been pursuing their statutory responsibility of aiding the
social and economic well-being of the National Park is one to which
the answer will vary depending on whose well-being is being
considered. The Section 52 policy seems to be most secure in a
legal sense when the presumption is made that no new houses should
be built in the Park. The agreements then allow sufficient
exceptions to be made to meet local need and create the planning
benefits set out in the Joint Structure Plan. It must be a matter of
debate whether a policy based on exceptions to the legal presumption
of no development is desirable as a blanket policy, even in those
places where the infrastructure to support development exists
already.

Perhaps the irony is that the policy has been overtaken by events.
The real sector of locally occupied, cheaper houses will be the
council houses sold at discount under the Housing Act, 1980. At
least two of the District Councils in the Park (Allerdale and South
Lakeland) are strongly opposed to such sales but whatever their
merits, these will do more than Section 52 agreements to aid
marginal house purchasers (House of Commons Environment Committee,
1980). The Section 52 policy will be of little benefit to the
better-off council tenants in this context and, of course, of even
less benefit to the poorer council tenants who would not expect to
buy a house under any circumstances. It is particularly interesting
to note that Section 19 of the Housing Act gives the local authorities in the Park the power either to buy back the house if it is
subsequently sold, or to place a covenant on the house so that it can

only be sold to full-time residents employed locally. The district
councils can therefore stop their former houses leaking into the
second home and retirement markets which was a very real possibility
in the Park. These powers - essentially Section 52 agreements
applied to council house sales - may act as a precedent, increasing
the chances of the Section 52 policy being approved. A similar
system of discrimination in favour of local people also operates in
the points systems used by the district councils to allocate council
houses. The main difference however is that in the public sector,
the houses belong to the council whereas Section 52 agreements are
being imposed by those who do not own the houses.

The conclusion would seem to be that, whatever the possible
weaknesses of the Section 52 policy, it is very difficult to see an
alternative policy given fewer publicly funded houses, the
separation of the Special Planning Board from the district council
housing authorities and the apparent assumption locally and
nationally that in future there must be more owner-occupation and
stronger protection of the landscape with fewer new houses. The
Special Planning Board's options were further narrowed by the
decision to meet the housing needs of local people not by helping
needy households directly, but indirectly by concentrating on private
sector houses only. The policy also experiences the difficulty
common to many planning authorities of the reification of a 'local
need' which it is so hard to conceptualise, define or measure under
current conditions of commuting and occupational mobility. The
separation for planning purposes of the Lake District from the rest
of Cumbria, of which it is such an integral part economically, is
also a handicap.

4.6   RECENT DEVELOPMENTS

In August 1981, the Secretary of State for the Environment
circulated his draft modifications to the Joint Structure Plan for
Cumbria and the Lake District National Park. He recommended that the
policy of restricting new housing should be continued. New houses
would only be permitted where all of the following conditions held.

a. the proposed site lies within the confines of existing
   development;

b. the proposed development will fulfil requirements arising
   from local reductions in average household size, or natural
   growth of the existing population, or the creation of new
   job opportunities in or adjacent to the National Park for
   which the provision of housing in the settlement concerned
   is appropriate;   and

c. the proposed houses are of a type and density which is
   appropriate both to the needs of the local population and
   to the character of the settlement.

The policy to restrict new housing for the occupation of locally employed, full-time residents is to be deleted. The Panel which examined the Structure Plan in public supported the local needs policy but the Secretary of State felt that it was "an unreasonable use of planning powers", "impracticable and inappropriate". He argued that "planning is concerned with the merits of the use of land, not the identity or merits of the occupiers. Planning permission for a particular use of land otherwise suitable for that use cannot appropriately be refused simply because the planning authority wish to restrict the user". This verdict is similar to one given for the Peak Park Structure Plan. Clearly planning is about land use and not land users. The Secretary of State recommends that local housing needs be met under the Housing Acts, that is, by the district councils and not by the Lake District Special Planning Board. The pressures on rural housing are likely to increase rather than decrease since the preliminary results of the 1981 Census show that between 1971 and 1981 the population of Cumbria increased by 1.5 per cent from 476,133 to 483,427 compared with an increase of only 0.5 per cent forecast in the Structure Plan. Although some commentators have detected a slowing down in the rate at which people take on second homes, there is little evidence of this in the Lake District. The four parishes of Borrowdale, Patterdale, Eskdale and Kentmere, which Bennett surveyed in particular detail in 1976, were re-surveyed in 1980. Every house was visited and second and holiday homes together formed 31 per cent of the housing stock of these parishes, second homes alone comprising 17 per cent. Nearly 20 per cent of the occupiers of second homes had taken up occupation within the five years prior to the survey. The specific tactic of using Section 52 agreements may well not survive but the pressures which have created the problem of meeting local housing needs are still as insistent as ever. Other methods of refusing planning permission could be tried.

If time proves this experiment in planning for housing in the Lake District to have been less than perfect, perhaps one should look less at the planning itself and more at the administrative and financial conditions within which it has had to be carried out. The relationship between planning and housing policies is neither simple nor obvious and it is helpful to examine the experiences of other areas to see how they have tackled the task of planning for housing in the countryside and then suggest some alternatives for the Lake District.

5. Alternative Housing Strategies

'How blessed is he who leads a country life,
  Unvexed with anxious cares, and void of strife!'
    John Dryden (1631-1700) <u>Epistles to John Driden of Chesterton.</u>

The provision of housing in the Lake District is an acutely difficult
process to regulate because of the considerable number of objectives
being pursued simultaneously. It is particularly difficult to help
local people to buy a house - however you define 'local' - when there
is a severe reduction on aesthetic grounds in the number of houses
granted planning permission, in addition to a reduction in the number
of new houses built by public finance and a reduction in the size of
the stock of council houses through sales. Nevertheless a desire to
assist local people and low-income households to obtain accommodation
is found very widely not only in Britain but also elsewhere. It is
therefore useful to examine how some other authorities have tried to
solve the problem since alternative strategies for the Lake District
may be found in other regions. Three broad strategies can be
detected. One is to control land use, another is to subsidise local
people and a third is to provide extra finance for publicly-financed
housing.

5.1 LAND-USE APPROACHES

   Controlling land use so as to promote local housing is the policy
currently pursued in the Lake District. However, it is difficult to
determine which group should have **privileged** access to such new
houses as are built. In Norway there is a system of land-use zoning
which was born of the rapid expansion of second homes in the upland
areas of Central Norway between Oslo and Trondhjem. The higher
standard of living in Norway had raised the number of households with
a second home to over twenty per cent and there was considerable
disquiet as purpose-built second homes sprang up further and further
afield from the main centres of population. This was partly a
product of the desire by many Norwegians for solitude and was partly
aided by improvements to the rather poor Norwegian road system. Huts
for second homes, often painted red and white, spread from the lower
coniferous forest up into the birch forest and then beyond on to the
high treeless fjell. This moorland area was ecologically sensitive
since damage to the plant cover would take a long time to recover
because of the slow rate of growth of plants in the cold climate.

The area was also aesthetically sensitive since buildings on the fjell in addition to the traditional seters (mountain huts for farmers in summer) were visible over a wide area. Servicing new buildings was also expensive since they were the furthest from the existing roads and electricity supplies. The rate of building was highest in accessible areas where the land belonged to low-income farmers. Jointly owned and state owned land was developed less rapidly.

In 1965 the Norwegian Government passed two Acts, one - the Building Act - to introduce physical planning and the other to prevent private fencing and building near the shore and in the mountains (Thormodsaeter, 1965 p.76). The latter was opposed by farmers many of whom wished to move into tourism to supplement their incomes. While outright restriction of development would have been costly for the Norwegian Government since compensation would have had to be paid (unlike in Britain), the needs of conservation had to be met and the compromise was to allow development of cabins for holiday makers only below the tree line. Here the provision of services is cheaper, the huts are less ecologically damaging and the trees provide a natural screen to prevent them being too obvious. The farmers meanwhile can still gain extra income from tourism.

The same principle of channelling second homes into areas which can cope with them, rather than stopping the growth of second homes altogether, has been followed in Denmark. Again a high standard of living and easy communication across a small country led to the rapid spread of second homes. This time the concern was over farmland and how this could be protected both for the benefit of farmers as food producers and for the benefit of the national balance of payments. In 1969 the Danish Parliament passed the Urban and Rural Zones Act which it had rejected six years earlier. This extended land-use planning across all rural areas and divided the country into three zones, namely urban, rural and for summer-houses. In rural areas there was to be no non-agricultural development nor any conversion of agricultural buildings although buildings of no agricultural value could be converted to industrial or commercial use. In the relatively small summer-house zones second homes could be built, these areas being selected so that the damage summer-houses were believed to cause to farming communities was minimized (Holmes, 1973).

In so far as second homes and, to a lesser extent, retirement homes are seen as a mixed blessing, it might be possible to avoid the difficulties inherent in attempting to reduce their growth and instead control their location more carefully. Rather than a blanket policy for the whole National Park, the construction of speculative housing, which might be bought by anyone, could be permitted only in those parts of the Park capable of taking extra people. The larger towns and villages such as Windermere and Keswick might be open to general building subject to land suitable for building being available. More sensitive areas where building

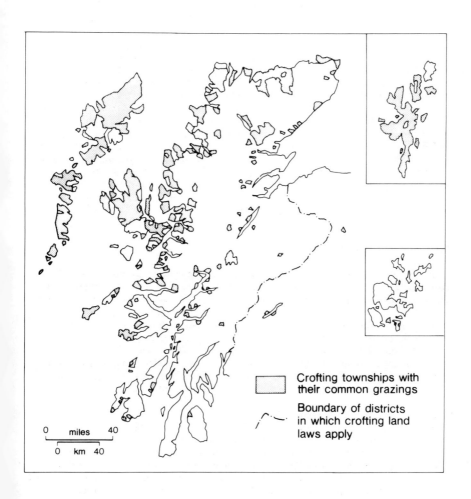

FIG.26.   Crofters' common grazings in Scotland (after Coull, 1968).

would harm either the landscape or the local community in some way,
would be off-limits to new house building even if land and infrastructure were available. The weakness of this policy would be the
same as for the current Section 52 policy in that there would be no
power to prevent the existing housing stock becoming second homes or
retirement homes. The policy would however allow more development
than there is currently on the grounds that the aesthetic case
against almost any new development seems difficult to sustain for
the entire Park. The Park is an administrative unit but is definitely not uniform in its landscape, socio-economic character or its
proportion of second homes. The current policy has a rough justice
to it and an administrative neatness, but it is thereby difficult to
defend in any specific case which might arise. If its application
were spatially more discriminating, its justification would similarly
be more secure when challenged by any specific proposal for development. As well as making more sense, the policy could be more in tune
with the case-law approach to British planning where any general
power (such as Section 52 agreements) only has such force as
subsequent specific cases and appeals reveal it to have.

5.2 SUBSIDISING PEOPLE

One of the alternatives to a land-use approach to rural housing
concentrates on the poorer house-buyer directly. The current policy
in the Lake District only helps the marginal house-buyer in so far as
it cuts out external demand and so might reduce house prices though
the scale of the latter effect is debatable. If it were desired to
help poorer people obtain houses - newly married couples in rather
low-pay industries, for example - then it is possible to find cases
where aid has been channelled specifically to this group and at a
predictable cost to the funding authority - neither being a feature
of the current housing policy in the Lake District.

The Northern and Western Isles of Scotland and much of the
Highlands are a case in point. They have been subject to a
distinctive form of land tenure known as crofting tenure since 1886
(Figure 26). Since 1897 grants have been available to crofters to
aid them with farm buildings and since 1949 aid with building or
improving houses has also been available. The landowners either did
not or could not provide sufficient housing for their crofter tenants,
despite the considerable size of their holdings (Figure 27). The
situation was exacerbated by the high density of the rural
population as population increase outstripped even the high rates of
out-migration. Unlike most British rural areas the crofting
population rose throughout the nineteenth century whereas elsewhere
it had been falling (Figure 28). The very small size of the farms
(most were under 10 hectares and a majority were less than 5
hectares in extent), the severe environment and the distance from
national markets combined to create a low standard of living for many
crofters. In addition, the quality of housing in crofting areas was
very poor indeed, with widespread overcrowding and many houses
without the basic amenities. As late as 1971, 26.2 per cent of
houses in the Western Isles were below tolerable standard compared

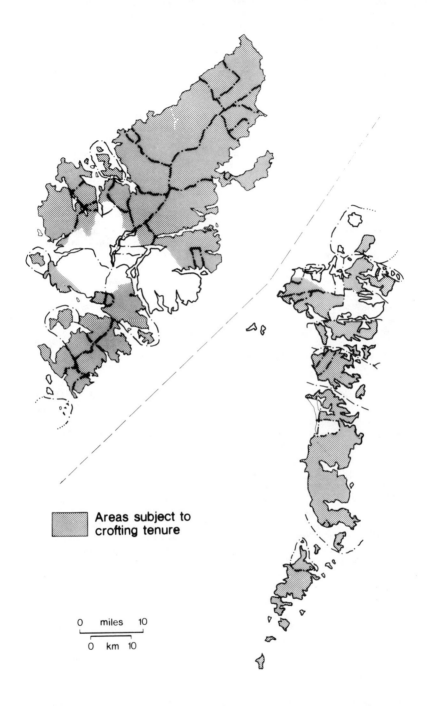

Areas subject to
crofting tenure

```
0    miles   10
0    km      10
```

FIG.27.   Landownership units in the Western Isles in ca. 1970
         (after Millman, 1970)

with 13.7 per cent for Scotland as a whole with the rural areas
outside Stornoway (population 5,152) having the poorest housing (as
Table 21 shows) despite at least 60 years of falling population.

The relatively satisfactory state of housing in Stornoway - the
only town in the Western Isles - is related to the high proportion of
houses there (nearly 58 per cent) which are rented from the local
authority and which conform to the tolerable standard criteria used
in the census. Even here, however, deficiencies exist since 95 per
cent of the council's houses built before 1939 and 52 per cent of the
post-war ones need extensive repairs or upgrading to their electrical
or kitchen facilities.

In the rural parishes, where the proportion of council houses never
rises above twenty per cent, the standards in owner-occupied housing
are very poor. Housing in the Western Isles south of Lewis is
particularly deficient, as is the provision of many other facilities,
reflecting the interest taken in different areas of the Western Isles
by the local authorities responsible for its administration before
the reorganisation of local government in 1975. The councillors
elected for Lewis were a quite influential group in Ross and Cromarty
County Council and they secured funds for Lewis. The councillors for
Harris and the other islands were a numerically smaller and less
influential group and less money was spent there by Inverness-shire
County Council.

Two methods of improving housing have been tried in the Western
Isles, one being local authority improvement grants and the other,
crofters' housing grants. The former have been available in the
Western Isles on comparable terms to those elsewhere in Great
Britain since the Housing Act, 1957. Nationally, eighty per cent of
improvement grants were given to owner-occupiers. The crofters'
housing grants were specific to the crofting districts of Scotland
and as such largely excluded towns like Stornoway. It is clear from
Table 22 that while the large number of sub-standard houses in the
landward parts of Lewis were being tackled vigorously by these two
schemes, the poor housing elsewhere (notably Barra) was not receiving
assistance commensurate with the scale of the problem. The poor
uptake of the 50 per cent local authority improvement grants has been
tentatively explained as being because the maximum grant of £1,850
was still a long way short of the sum needed to improve the average
sub-standard house in, for example, Barra where construction costs
were higher than in Lewis.

The degree of assistance given to crofters after 1976 for building
and improving houses is set out in Table 23. Until 1980, building
materials for construction could be bought from stores run by the
Department of Agriculture and Fisheries for Scotland which reduced
the transport component in the cost of building materials. Between
1949 when grants first became available and 1979, £4,724,429 was paid
to crofters in the Highlands and Islands to build or improve 6,887
houses, about 38 per cent of the new and improved houses and about

Population Change 1801–1971 Scotland and Western Isles

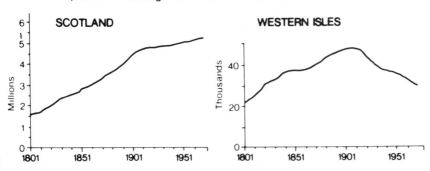

Population Change 1801–1971 Lewis, Harris and Stornoway small burgh

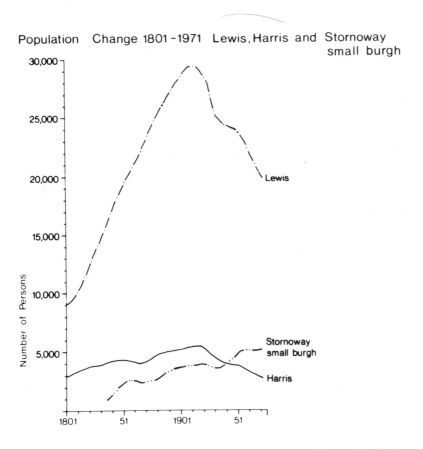

FIG. 28.   Population trends in the Western Isles, 1801–1971 (after
Comhairle nan Eilean 1976).

TABLE 21. Household amenities in 1971 in Western Isles and Scotland.

Area	Number of households lacking exclusive use of 3 amenities*	Sub-standard houses as percentage of total households
Stornoway	105	6.8
Lewis (landward)	1160	24.5
Harris	365	38.2
N. Uist	225	43.7
S. Uist	340	35.6
Barra	190	49.4
Western Isles	2385	26.2
Scotland	230735	13.7

*The three amenities referred to are hot water, fixed bath and inside W.C.

Source: Census of Population (1971) and Comhairle nan Eilean (1976) p.42.

119

TABLE 22. Distribution of sub-standard houses and housing grants in the Western Isles.

Area	Percentage of the Western Isles' houses below tolerable standard (1971)	Percentage of crofters' housing built to replace BTS housing (1975)	Percentage of local authority improvement grants (1975/6)
Stornoway	3.4	0.0	5.5
Lewis (landward)	40.7	73.5	76.6
Harris	13.1	8.2	9.4
North Uist	11.1	4.1	2.3
South Uist	18.4	14.3	6.3
Barra	13.2	0.0	0.0
Western Isles	100	100	100

Source: Comhairle nan Eilean (1976) pp.43-4.

TABLE 23. Crofters' housing grants after 1976

	Maximum grant	Maximum loan	Loan rate of interest
New house	£4,000	£5,500	$3\frac{1}{8}$%
Improved house	£750	£4,000	$3\frac{1}{8}$%

Source: Department of Agriculture and Fisheries for Scotland (1976).

33 per cent of the grants paid being in the Western Isles between
1951 and 1975 (DAFS, 1980 p.27 and Comhairle nan Eilean, 1976 p.43).
Even these quite generous grants and low-interest loans were not
enough to cover the full cost of a new house, of course, and the
crofter in Lewis might have to find at least £3,000 from his own
resources to pay for the house. In the southern islands the
shortfall could be up to £10,000. Loans from banks and mortgages
from building societies were also more difficult to obtain since the
crofter had no heritable security (few owned their croft before 1976)
although the position of crofters vis-à-vis building societies has
improved recently. Even when allowance is made for some artificial
inflation of house prices because of the grant, there is still a gap
to be bridged for the poorer sections of the community. However,
given the very high level of owner-occupation in an area of low
average earnings, the generous crofting grants and the low-interest
loans were a major stimulus to improving the quality of housing for
the predominant agricultural section of the rural community. They
have not, of course, helped people in poor quality houses who are not
crofters and it is clear that there remain major problems to be
tackled by Housing Action Areas and other localised measures
instigated by the local authority.

A more broadly based system of subsidy operates in West Germany
where local government will pay a subsidy to the owner of rented
property to allow him to rent it at a lower cost to a low-income
family. The only equivalent to this in Britain is the rent and rates
rebates which may be given to very poor families receiving supplementary benefit. The German scheme is however much wider in scope
and in the income range over which it operates and it has the merit
of producing socially mixed blocks of flats with subsidised and
unsubsidised tenants housed together. In effect, it is families in
need which are being subsidised rather than houses for the possibly
needy as with the financing of British council house building. In
Canada home ownership for the marginal house-buyer is subsidised by
an interest-free Government loan to low-income families to supplement
what they can borrow from private financial institutions. Since 1978
there has also been a system whereby mortgage repayments could be
reduced by decreasing amounts for ten years by which time inflation
will be reducing the real value of the full repayments.

An alternative scheme of subsidy operates in the Isle of Man which
is faced with problems not dissimilar to those in the Lake District.
Here too is an attractive area rather smaller than the Lake District
though with a higher population (60,000 compared with 46,000 in the
Lake District) where scenery and the tourist trade attract visitors
who may wish to stay permanently. They are also attracted no doubt
by the very low rate of income tax in the island which is internally
self-governing. The marginal rate of income tax, after deduction of
allowances, is 20 per cent. Domestic rates are also lower in the Isle
of Man than in the United Kingdom. Not surprisingly, many people who
would pay higher rates of tax in the United Kingdom seek Manx
residential status and consequently there is a strong external demand

for houses and the prices of houses is generally higher than in the
United Kingdom. House prices have also been subject to the same
inflationary pressure as on the mainland as Figure 29 shows.

The consequence of this is that in an area of relatively high
owner-occupation - 53 per cent of houses were owner-occupied in 1971
compared with 49 per cent in the United Kingdom - the active
programme of council house building has not been enough to meet the
housing aspirations of the Manx people (Isle of Man Government, 1980
p.113). In 1971, 21 per cent of the housing stock was publicly owned
and since then an even higher percentage of completed houses -
about 27 per cent - has been in the public sector. The Isle of Man
Government has attempted to bridge the gap between public rented
housing and the rather expensive private sector by instituting a
series of schemes to subsidise owner-occupation particularly for the
lower income group. The scheme only applies to Manx residents
(employees or businessmen) which excludes the second-home and
retirement groups and it is not available for the purchase of large
houses nor for people deemed to have sufficient income to buy a house
without help. The assistance under the current scheme - the House
Purchase Scheme, 1978 - is very generous since both a grant and a
loan may be given. A grant of up to 10 per cent of the purchase
price or valuation of the house can be given up to a maximum of
£1,250 for those with a gross income of under £3,500 in 1980. The
grant is less for those with higher incomes and no grant is payable
if the applicant's income is over £4,000.

The other form of assistance is a loan scheme which counterbalances
the complete lack of mortgage facilities from building societies on
the Island. The Government loans are given on very favourable terms
since they can cover 100 per cent of the valuation or purchase price
up to a maximum of £18,000 and repayment can take place over a period
up to 40 years or until retirement age. This potentially long period
of repayment aims to reduce the monthly repayments particularly in
the first few years of the mortgage before inflation has reduced the
real value of the repayments. The ceiling of £18,000 corresponds to
the mean price in 1979 of a new house on the island. The most
attractive feature of the scheme is the low and stable rate of
interest charged on the loan. The maximum rate of interest in May
1980 was normally 9 per cent while for people with incomes under
£3,500 the rate was only 7 per cent. The corresponding interest
rates in the U.K. were 17 per cent base lending rate at the banks
and 15 per cent for most U.K. building societies' mortgages. No one
is allowed to spend more than one-third of their income on the
monthly repayments of interest and principal but with low interest
rates, low domestic rates and low income tax rates, this is still a
most generous system of subsidy, and it has appealed to the younger
people since 47 per cent of the successful applicants in 1979 were
under 30 years of age and 69 per cent were under 35 (Isle of Man
Government, 1980 p.122). The current scheme's predecessors were
also successful since 3,686 loans were given under the House Advance
Scheme between 1967 and 1979 and another 778 loans for nearly

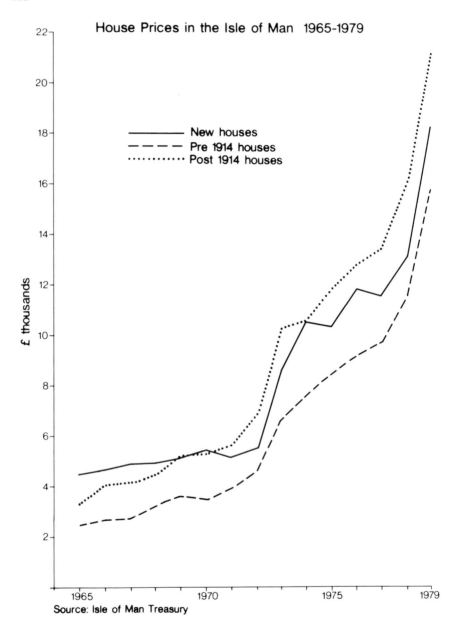

FIG.29.   House prices in the Isle of Man, 1965-79 (after Isle of
Man Government, 1980).

£3 million were given under the Building by Private Enterprise Scheme
(Isle of Man Government, 1980 pp. 120-1). The Manx Government did
attempt to build houses itself at St. John's which it sold to Manx
residents but the scheme was not repeated. Although the general
trend in all house building on the Island has been steadily downward
over several years as in the United Kingdom (Figure 30), the Manx
government has used council housing and subsidised credit for house
purchase by residents as the twin methods of meeting the housing
needs of local people who cannot obtain housing unaided.

The Manx Government has been faced with the same problem as in the
Lake District of an external demand for housing inflating house
prices and they have taken full advantage of their island position,
and their political and financial autonomy. No area or local
authority in Great Britain could have such powers and neither of the
major political parties would wish any local authority to be able to
so blunt the centralised power of national government. The Manx
schemes recognise and encourage owner-occupation among Manx residents
with extra help for the lower income groups and with a back-up of
public housing for those who cannot contemplate even subsidised house
purchase or who choose not to spend their money buying a house. In
Britain owner-occupation is also subsidised through mortgage interest
relief for tax payers, but unlike the Manx scheme this gives greatest
assistance to those on the highest tax rates - for a person with a
marginal tax rate of 50 per cent the effective rate of interest on a
mortgage in Britain is halved. The Manx scheme is more surely
directed at the marginal house purchaser, is more cost effective in
terms of houses bought versus tax revenue lost, and so is less
regressive.

An even more extreme case can be found in the housing policy in the
Channel Islands which demonstrates that helping local people
indirectly by reducing external demand rather than by helping the low
paid can have unexpected consequences. A warmer climate than the
Isle of Man and similarly low income tax rates have created a large
potential demand for houses in the main islands of Jersey and
Guernsey. These are, however, small islands with population
densities 7 and 10 times greater respectively than the Isle of Man
and they have been faced with a relatively greater inflow of
residents in proportion to the land available. Their system of
control has acted to stem the inflow rather than, as in the Manx
case, to subsidise the local population who wished to buy a house.
In effect the legislation controlling access to housing has been
used as an immigration policy which has divided people into three
groups. First, there are the residents who can buy any house they
wish. Second there are the "external workers", that is, people
whose professional or technical skills are required on the island.
This group may obtain a licence to obtain a house. If they change
house or job, they may be required to leave the island. In Jersey,
this group obtain resident status, and so unfettered access to
housing, after they have lived on the island for ten years. In
Guernsey they obtained resident status after 10 years up to 1973

124

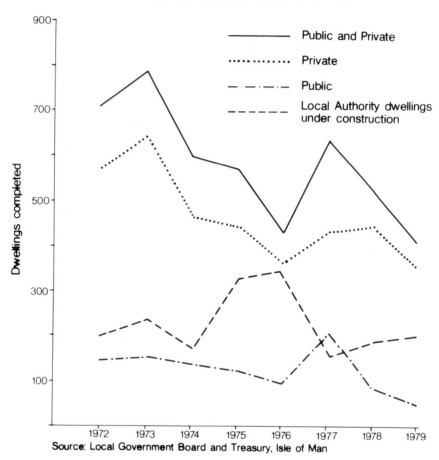

New Dwellings Completed in the Isle of Man

— Public and Private

.... Private

— · — · — Public

— — — — Local Authority dwellings
under construction

Source: Local Government Board and Treasury, Isle of Man

FIG.30.   New dwellings completed in the Isle of Man, 1972-9 (after
Isle of Man Government, 1980).

and since 1975 the law states that this group can never gain
residential status. They will always live as licence holders,
subject to expulsion if their employment circumstances change. The
third group are the prospective immigrants, mostly from the United
Kingdom. In Jersey there has existed for a long time an open market
of houses which immigrants can buy and a closed market for local
residents. Needless to say, the houses on the open market have been
much more expensive - the minimum price in 1975 being £50,000.

As immigration to Jersey increased, an additional restriction
was imposed in 1971 in that the immigrants had to be wealthy enough
to pay at least £2,000 income tax and in 1973 this requirement was
raised successively to £10,000. With a marginal tax rate of 20 per
cent, this implied an annual gross income of at least £50,000.
Jersey required immigrants to be both wealthy and have high incomes
whereas previously wealth was deemed sufficient qualification. Even
this limit was not felt to be reducing the inflow sufficiently since
in the United Kingdom the effective marginal tax for people with
investment incomes of over £1 million was over 90 per cent. In 1975
the requirement for entry to Jersey was tightened so that only 15
people a year would be allowed in, each with an annual liability to
Jersey taxation of over £10,000, that is an income of over £50,000.
Relevant considerations for the selection of the lucky 15 included
family size, number of house staff to be employed and whether any
business was to be transacted on the island. In Guernsey no such tax
qualification is applied, and the income only has to be able to buy
an open market house whose price is unlikely to be under £50,000.

The difficulty the islands have is that this immigrant group of
about 1100 people on Jersey contributes some 30 per cent of all tax
revenue so they must not be frightened off, whereas the need for
slow population growth and fear of being swamped by immigrants,
particularly strong on Guernsey, have to be met. The Jersey
proposal for the tax liability test originated from their new
economic advisor Mr. Colin Powell. During debates in the States of
Jersey in 1974, it was proposed that only £150,000 worth of new
settlers a year be allowed. Although this proposal was defeated as
being too overtly mercenary for good public relations, it identifies
the underlying theme in Jersey of maintaining just sufficient
immigration to maintain tax revenue and so help keep down the tax
rate for residents and new settlers alike. In Guernsey the concern
has been more to create a single qualification for residence based on
one's birth in Guernsey or one's parents birth there and in addition
living there. Provision also had to be made for émigré Guernsey
people to return without undue strain on the island's land resources.
It is difficult to feel sympathy for extremely wealthy people who can
no longer gain access to these tax havens in the same numbers as
previously. However the insecurity of residence for specialist
workers is considerable since they are all, in effect, living in tied
housing. They can live in Jersey and Guernsey only for so long as
their services are required. The policies of the Channel Islands are
an interesting example of how internal self-government, high

population density and low taxation can weld together housing and immigration measures into a single discriminatory policy in favour of local people which one would hope could not be repeated elsewhere in the United Kingdom. The lesson from this study of the Channel Islands is that housing policy affects migration even when this is not its overt intention and 'meeting local need' can become a justification for discrimination which may become questionable.

5.3 MORE PUBLICLY FUNDED HOUSING

The third major tactic which has been adopted to provide low cost housing, this time for rent, is through the use of housing associations. Unlike local authorities they do not have a continuing remit to house everyone in an area who asks for shelter. Instead they tap an additional source of usually national finance to build extra houses to meet more tightly circumscribed areas of need. They can either be national or local in their scale of operation. The largest in Britain is the Scottish Special Housing Association (S.S.H.A.).

This was set up in 1937 as the Scottish Special Areas Housing Association Ltd. and as its name implies it is a centrally funded agency building houses for rent in areas of need. The average rent in a S.S.H.A. house is currently (1981) 14 per cent higher than the rent charged by local authorities which, when controlled by the Labour Party, tend to subsidise council house rents from the rates. Originally the S.S.H.A. only operated in the 'Special Areas' of particularly high unemployment but since 1945 it has been able to build in any area the Secretary of State for Scotland saw as in need of extra houses. The S.S.H.A. works with the co-operation of the local authority and operates in priority areas designated by the Secretary of State for Scotland. It has supplemented the local authorities' house building in areas with much poor quality housing (e.g. Glasgow and the coalfields) and in areas receiving overspill population from Glasgow. It has built houses in areas where there have been a rapid increase in housing demand due to industrial development (e.g. the Grangemouth oil refinery and the former car assembly plant at Linwood). It has also contributed to the supply of new houses in the areas affected by North Sea Oil development in north east Scotland and the Moray Firth district. The S.S.H.A. now rents over 90,000 houses with the guiding principle being that it operates in an area until the local authority by itself can meet the need for cheaper housing. It can change its priorities quickly and so is a flexible agent of policy, yet there are difficulties. It cannot subsidise its rents from the rates as local authorities can, but equally it cannot let rents get too far out of line with those of council houses since there will be resistance from tenants. Central government may have to subsidise S.S.H.A. rents but the cost to the Exchequer needs to be limited otherwise the case for abolishing the S.S.H.A. and transferring its function to the councils is strengthened. There is no reason why such a system could not be applied to pressured rural areas such as the English Lake District as well as areas of greater need such as the inner cities so as to reduce council house waiting lists more quickly. However there is no likelihood of such an organisation being set up in the immediate future for England, nor indeed of local authorities being given the money to do the equivalent.

Housing associations need not, of course, be national in their remit. They can be local organisations and the earliest housing associations in the eighteenth and nineteenth centuries were local organisations and privately funded. Most of the Victorian housing associations have ceased to operate and the second wave of housing associations which were formed under the Industrial and Provident Societies Act of 1893-4 remained very small scale in their housing provision. After the Second World War housing associations concentrated on housing for special groups such as the elderly or handicapped. By this time, funding was available from the local authorities which could nominate some or all of the tenants. The post-war period was marked by diversification in the housing associations with considerable variety in their areas of operation, their organisation and the type of housing provided. Variation was increased further after 1964 when funding for housing associations was both expanded and centralised through the Housing Corporation. Ten years later the Housing Corporation acquired further powers since it was required to supervise the constitution and organisation of all housing associations to which it lent money.

Although housing associations provided only about two per cent of all housing in 1980, they have been building between one-fifth and one-quarter of all new houses and the proportion of house improvements attributable to them is even higher. In the Lake District they have had limited impact, except in the parts of Allerdale and Copeland districts which are in the National Park, where the North East Housing Association (established in the same period as the Scottish Special Housing Association) provides 10 and 56 per cent respectively of all public housing. Their houses are mostly outside Keswick and so they perform a most valuable function complementary to the local authorities' housing provision which is mostly in Keswick itself. The N.E.H.A. has been nominated by Allerdale and Copeland District Councils to carry out work for them and, in return, the councils have the sole nomination rights for the Association's houses. In South Lakeland the Abbeyfield Society provides 84 residential units for the elderly and the Lake District Housing Association provides 27 sheltered residences in Windermere. Both are examples of small specialist associations. There are also many other very small associations in South Lakeland with under ten houses each, most having distant origins in charitable organisations and alms houses. In Eden District, the Lowther Housing Association has provided 56 housing units in Lowther and Askham parishes in the area of the Lowther estate from which the association drew much of its initial inspiration and impetus. The association allocate their properties without reference to the local authority and their rents are a little higher than for council property.

128

The housing association movement is a useful device for supplement-
ing council housing and attracting extra money into the provision of
public rented property. Where they are catering for specialist need,
for example the elderly, their contribution is especially valuable not
only for the person directly concerned, but also since it may free
another house, perhaps too large for its occupant, which a bigger
family could occupy. Rogers (1981, p.194) has noted that the
proportion of under-occupied houses in the National Parks was above the
average for English rural districts in 1971 and the Lake District Park
was not an exception. There is however disquiet over the housing
associations' ambivalent status as private bodies funded from the
public purse. Doubt has been expressed over the financial account-
ability of some of the 3,000 housing associations in Great Britain and
whether their criteria for allocating properties are entirely
equitable. However, it can also be claimed that housing associations
are small-scale organisations without the bureaucratic inertia of
local government and so they may be able to identify housing needs
more clearly and react more rapidly.

5.4 SOME ALTERNATIVES FOR THE LAKE DISTRICT

Before alternatives can be suggested, the general assumptions and
framework within which housing is to be provided have to be specified.
It is assumed that one of the objectives of housing policy is to
assist those who cannot obtain adequate housing solely with their own
resources and to do so with the minimum expenditure and having regard
to both the maintenance of the landscape of the Lake District and the
interests of those who can afford to buy a house. Four alternatives
come to mind.

The first alternative is to build more houses in the Lake District,
both council housing and private, so as to counteract any inflationary effect on house prices of the current policy. Even the Treasury
favours advance house building as a means of attracting industry so
making the countryside cheaper to service (Treasury, 1976 p.25).
Council house building in rural areas is usually limited because it
is more expensive for each house than in urban areas due to longer
travelling times for builders, Parker-Morris standards of
construction and the design constraints needed for areas of
attractive landscape. The cost could be reduced by building houses
only in bigger estates where overheads could be spread over more
houses. The abolition of Parker-Morris standards may help to cheapen
council houses but a larger grant from central government would be
the quickest way to get more council houses in the countryside. This
implies a policy of concentrating public housing in a few places,
probably the larger towns, and as such represents a form of key
settlement policy for the lower paid implemented through housing
provision. The trade-off is between some redistribution of council-
house tenants into larger settlements, against longer commuting for
those of them who work in the countryside. Scattering council houses
more widely may increase the cost of each house and reduce the number
that can be built thus promoting depopulation. A concern to help the

largest number of people in the Park is taking policy objectives back to those of the 1960s which seem to have been too rapidly discarded. More private housing for whoever wishes it could and should be allowed in the larger settlements where infrastructure permits, since this will have only the slightest effect on the landscape of the Lake District if the houses are carefully designed and sited. Nothing that is done in the way of planning in the Lake District will stop people wishing to retire to the Lakes or have a second home there and the consequences of restricting the supply of new houses may be worse than the original ailment. Rather one could adopt a land-use policy based more on the Danish and Norwegian examples of channelling new houses into the areas which can best absorb them. It may be that the Danes and Norwegians chose this redistributional policy because, at the time, restricting development left them open to claims for compensation, unlike in Britain. However there would be merit in a more geographically aware policy, rather than a blanket one for the variety of situations in the National Park.

In the mid-1970s the Special Planning Board had argued themselves into a dilemma. Development (including housing) had to be reduced since development harmed the landscape. The local people needed to be helped to find housing in the Park but building more houses was seen as contrary to the protection of the landscape. From this emerged the policy of reserving most new housing for local people. Yet the dilemma was more apparent than real. Is it true that stronger protection of the landscape demands less development? It probably does when one is concerned with forestry, new roads, silos, hedgerow removal, building design and the siting of caravan sites. But does it apply to new housing? The essence of the Lake District may be open fells and quaint roads but it does not include a lack of houses. One may have to control the siting and design of houses - that is accepted throughout Britain - but how new houses of appropriate design and siting can harm the landscape is not clear. If one then removes the argument that restricting new housing aids conservation of the Lake District, the dilemma which produced the local needs policy disappears and many more options for helping local people obtain housing become possible. The policy should then be a flexible one of rigorously preventing unsuitable housing while liaising with local housing authorities to promote as much housing as possible where it will produce significant social benefits.

A second alternative would be to continue the policy of almost no new housing of any kind in the Park and put all the new housing outside the Park. This would be reasonable if the Park's economy could be maintained, with adequate facilities for commuting by public and private transport into the Park. Like borrowing money to build council houses, this would be a continuing commitment for many decades, but it would have the advantage over the first strategy of recognising fully the aesthetic argument against building in the Lake District National Park. There would also need to be a sufficient supply of houses for rent outside the Park which might acquire a museum-like quality rather than continue as a balanced community.

A third alternative would be to leave housing provision for poorer employees to their employer. If the farmer, shopkeeper or hotelier needs full-time rather than seasonal workers then he should either pay them enough to rent or buy a house on the open market or provide housing. As already discussed, the tied cottage was an institution open to abuse and excessively deferential relationships between employer and employee. Yet in a situation such as is found in the Lake District, it has the merit of linking a specific person in a low-pay industry to a specific job. There is a directness about this policy which is appealing, but only if the ending of the contract of employment does not lead to homelessness. Many seasonal staff in hotels and shops may not wish to remain in the Lake District during the winter. There is already an increase in the council waiting lists at the end of the tourist season, as hotel staff find themselves homeless and again in the spring, as families in holiday accommodation are evicted before the start of the tourist season, a pattern Larkin has noted in Dorset (Larkin 1979, pp. 74-8). The reaction of employers to having to provide more housing for their permanent employees could be to mechanise, particularly in farming, or to use more family labour or self-service methods, so reducing employment in the Lakes. If housing provision altered employment in this way it would be the tail wagging the dog.

The fourth alternative would be for financial aid to be given to the lower income groups to counteract the high cost of housing in the Lake District. This tactic would accept that the attractiveness of the Lake District is bound to lead to a higher cost of living including higher house prices and rents and would then try and place the lower income groups in a better position to rent or buy property. This would depend on means-testing to determine financial eligibility, which poses formidable technical problems and usually generates heated opposition. There would also need to be a system of residential eligibility which would not be nearly as easy to establish in the Lake District as in the Isle of Man or Channel Islands. It would also depend on the assumption that this subsidy would not be translated into higher prices for lower priced accommodation which could lead to a pointless and expensive spiral of subsidy and prices. There is some suspicion that this has already happened in the Western Isles since house prices were not controlled. The parallel case would be the price support subsidies given to farmers which, it is alleged, have led to inflated prices for land. The similarity between the land and housing markets is that, in both, supply is inelastic in the short term.

A mechanism for such subsidies already exists to a limited extent in the national system of rent and rate rebates which are allowed to lower-income tenants in the public and private sectors. In 1976 about 1.2 million households received such housing allowances, compared with 5.5 million households in receipt of tax relief on mortgage interest payments (Cullingworth 1979, p.140). In addition, the nationally applied system of option mortgages allows government to pay building societies a subsidy so that marginal house buyers (who are not

taxpayers and so not eligible for the full tax relief on a mortgage)
can obtain a mortgage at a rate of interest below the market rate.
When the normal mortgage rate was 11.75 per cent, for example, the
option mortgage rate was 7.95 per cent (Boddy 1980, p.53).   This
system reduces the heavy initial cost of a mortgage and compensates
for this by raising the repayments in later years. By then, of
course, inflation of earnings should counteract in real terms the
increase in repayments. The proportion of option mortgages rose to
20 per cent of all mortgages in 1972 and then declined to 11 per cent
in 1978 as fiscal drag increased the number of taxpayers. These
schemes are not specifically rural in their application but they show
that the framework for systems of subsidy to purchasers and renters
of houses among the lower paid already exist. Whether it would be
administratively possible to give additional subsidy to the lower
paid in the countryside must be open to doubt however.

    Yet in a real sense these policies are on the wrong scale. Central
government provides subsidies to all households on a national basis
to stimulate house provision, yet the need for housing is best
identified at a local, perhaps even a parish level while the costs of
building houses vary spatially very much more than the government
subsidies or cost yard-sticks suggest. It would be possible to meet
this by varying the rates of rent and rate allowances by district or
even within districts. Whatever system of assistance for house
building is used ought to have a very local component to it.   It
would be a bold and useful experiment to give each parish council or
group of parish councils the power to borrow sufficient money to
build just one or two new houses each year to supplement the local
authority's efforts. The parish council would then allocate these
houses in consultation with the local authority. Such a system would
not be feasible in a city, since the scale of need there is better
tackled on a larger scale and parish or community councils have a
less intimate knowledge of specific housing needs. In rural areas,
however, it holds out the promise of invigorating parish administration and meeting housing needs as perceived locally. It might help
meet pockets of currently hidden need.

    The possibility therefore arises of a three-tiered system of
providing public housing, each tier corresponding to a given scale of
need.   There would be a national house-building agency similar to
the Scottish Special Housing Association which would build houses in
the areas of greatest need or where the local authority was
particularly hard pressed. Some rural areas might benefit from this
agency's work. The bulk of public housing would be provided by
local authorities as at present aided by higher building subsidies
and rent and rate rebates in areas of higher building costs, lower
incomes and high rents. A third tier of house building would be
added to meet the numerically small need for housing which slips
through the nets cast by local authority and national agencies. The
fact that the need in some parishes is numerically small is no reason
for not trying to meet that need with the same urgency as for the
inner-city. Rather it is an argument for a mechanism which can deploy

the small amount of resources needed in as effective a way as possible
for the benefit of the community. This arrangement need not mean that
more houses are built nationally, though the projected building
programme for the early 1980s looks very small at a time when the
subsidy of mortgage interest relief to house buyers is not being
reduced and the sale of council houses is building up. A three-tier
arrangement would however provide a closer match between need and
supply whatever the total volume of resources devoted to housing, so
that the stock of houses in the future will more closely meet the
changing requirements of the rural population without the practical
and theoretical shortcomings of enforced population concentration
through key settlement policy. If planning is to temper the more
regressive aspects of the free market by helping the lower paid
obtain housing, it cannot do so alone. Co-operation with housing
departments and a more active local and national programme to provide
local authority houses (by whatever means) will be needed.

5.5 THE LAKE DISTRICT AND NATIONAL POLICY

An examination of alternative strategies for a particular area must
also consider the possibility of a change in housing policy at
national level. It would be reasonable to expect that a housing
policy should be both equitable and efficient. Inefficiency leaves
open the possibility of extra assistance being given to some groups
or areas in particular need without raising the total cost of the
housing programme. One judgement on the equitability and efficiency
of the current national housing policy would be that it does well
enough but could do better. Although a lot is spent on housing aid,
it is a low proportion of the Gross National Product by European
standards. A very great deal has been achieved to raise the standard
of housing as measured by the age of the housing stock, amenities and
the number of houses. Yet the continuing high cost of subsidies to
owner-occupiers through mortgage interest relief raises the question
of whether the considerable proportion of the better-off who are
owner-occupiers ought to pay progressively less in real terms for a
house which, as time goes by, provides them with an asset of
increasing value and which, if sold, is an untaxed capital gain. The
scale of these tax reliefs is partly a function of inflation and fiscal drag rather than an intentional policy and they are particularly
valuable for both first-time buyers and for the low income owner-
occupiers (Figure 31). Yet it is arguable that a person on a high
marginal tax rate who bought a house ten years ago is getting his
housing too cheaply and could make a bigger contribution to housing
the poor. Nevertheless, the proliferation of housing subsidies at
nationally uniform rates to both owner-occupier and tenants of public
and private housing has reached such levels that its housing function
is almost overwhelmed by its economic and political significance.
Tax reliefs, fair rents and rent rebates are now so firmly embedded in
incomes policy that their contribution is defended on grounds of
political advantage and management of the national economy. Their
pervasive effects on housing demand and supply are largely secondary
to their effects on income distributions. Changing the current system

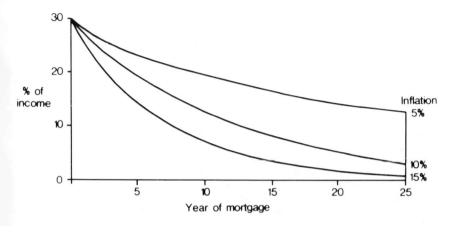

FIG.31.   Mortgage repayments as a proportion of income given
           different rates of inflation (after Boddy, 1980).

of subsidising everybody, but some more than others, is fraught with
difficulties, and entrenched opposition from political groups,
individuals, financial institutions and Departments of State usually
reduces reform to the most gradual of incremental change. The
similarity of Conservative and Labour views on how to deal with
housing has strengthened the hand of the proponents of the status
quo.

There has been a reduction over the last twenty years in the
formerly universal shortage of housing which has allowed the needs
of particular areas and groups to be brought into clearer focus.
Some groups such as the very poor, those in mobile homes and those
deemed less eligible on council waiting lists have not benefited as
much as many others from housing policy. It is quite easy to devise
ways of making houses cheaper to buy - low interest loans to buyers,
mortgage-interest tax relief, part-ownership of houses or subsidies
to builders. The methods are numerous but each has the effect of
helping all house buyers unless they are means-tested, of not
applying specific help to the local community and of tending to
raise house prices. The opportunity cost of the tax revenue forgone
by regressive mortgage allowances to all house buyers is considerable
and a decisive shift in emphasis is needed away from general house
provision to provision aimed more selectively at those areas and
groups which have been less well provided for by the current system.
Such a switch from a broad policy to a differentiated one requires
greater local initiatives as well as a back-up source of supply of
houses for areas of greater need. The Lake District is a
fascinating area to study but it must also be recognised how variable
British rural areas are in their housing. Dunn, Rawson and Rogers
(1980) used a cluster analysis to group local government districts in
England into seven types based on the tenure of houses, their
occupiers, and their physical condition (Figure 32). This variation
in conditions is also found in the even smaller areas which comprise
local government districts and for this reason, if no other, the
involvement of the lowest possible tier of local government in house
provision is desirable. In this way supply and demand may be more
closely matched than by the current local authority and private
enterprise systems alone.

The feature common to all these alternative strategies is that,
unlike the current policy, none could be operated entirely within
the framework of current legislation by any local planning authority
in Great Britain. Each would call for concerted action by more than
one department and local authority. This need for co-ordination is
a hurdle of no mean size and how it might be overcome will be
discussed in the next chapter. It is also clear that currently the
scope for local initiative is very restricted. Patently national
trends and problems are only marginally susceptible to local
solutions.

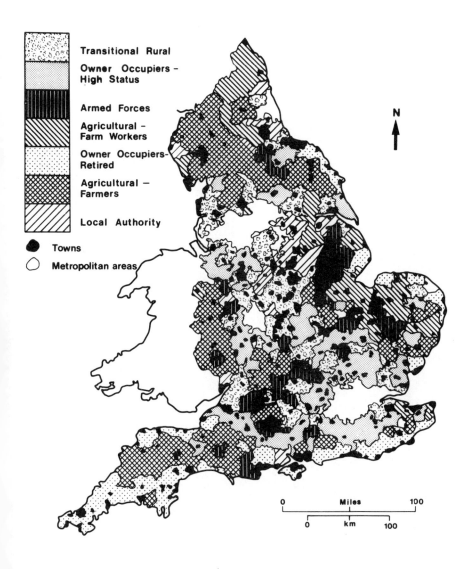

FIG. 32.   Types of rural area in England and Wales (after Dunn,
            Rawson and Rogers, 1980).

6. Conflicts in Rural Planning

'Home is the place where, when you have to go there,
They have to take you in.
                    I should have called it
Something you somehow haven't to deserve.'
                    R. Frost <u>The Death of the Hired Man</u> (1914)

The hired man in Frost's poem did not have a home of his own for most
of his life and, while a home as a right is an attractive proposition,
it has proved no easy matter to so arrange the supply of housing for
this to be possible. The difficulty stems partly from the cost of a
house. Even one of modest proportions is expensive to build and the
persistent negative skewness of income distributions means that many
cannot afford to buy or rent one without subsidy. There is also
unequal competition for the stock of houses between the richer and
poorer sections of the community. Most countries accept as fundamental
the private ownership of houses, even countries like Poland, Yugoslavia
and, to a very limited extent, the U.S.S.R. Many countries also
arrange their tax and credit systems so that some greater or lesser
financial encouragement is given to promote private home ownership.
Superimposed on this has been the continuing dispersal of city people
into the countryside. Some are trading off cheaper rural houses against
more expensive commuting, others come periodically as second-home
owners and many retire to the countryside after selling their town
house. Urban and rural housing markets in most of Great Britain have
merged into a single market embracing city and hinterland, as H.G.
Wells anticipated when writing at the turn of this century.

'Indeed it is not too much to say that the London citizen of
the year 2000 AD may have a choice of nearly all of England
and Wales south of Nottingham and east of Exeter as his suburb...'
                    (Wells, 1914 p.46).

These people come for all manner of reasons. They appreciate a
better environment for bringing up their children, cheaper housing or
a safer life than in the cities. They may come for peace of mind,
status or to be seen to be 'doing something for the village'.

'But it bears upon the question that ugliness and squalor upon
the main road will appeal to the more prosperous for remedy
with far more vigour than when they are stowed compactly in
a slum.'
                    (Wells, 1914 p.60).

They come because now they can come - car ownership is so high that commuting by car is now feasible for many families and the improvement in trunk roads and motorways has furthered these trends. Whatever their causes, there is no doubting the strength and persistence of the urbanization of the countryside nor the extent to which traditional rural occupations have declined in relative importance this century. These are perhaps more important than the statistics for the proportion of the workforce employed in agriculture would suggest. Wagstaff (1973) estimated that the work-force dependent on agriculture but not employed directly on farms, had been rising steadily and in Scotland was now between 1.6 and 2 times the size of the farm work-force.

There is no way a local planner can stop this urbanization of the countryside. He can turn a blind eye to it if the local planning committee is so minded or he can try and mitigate the trend, but he cannot halt it. The lesson of the Lake District experiment would seem to be that unless all house allocation and house prices are controlled, you cannot stop second-home owners and the retired coming to an area without the price mechanism causing distortions elsewhere in the housing market which may be worse than the original 'second-home problem.' This is particularly the case when there are so many people retiring to the Lakes, a general dearth of new housing which has it origins in central government policy and a growing concern for landscape protection. A planning policy based on the assumption of almost no development needs the most powerful case in its favour to be reasonable, particularly when so many changes of a social and economic character can take place outwith the Planning Acts.

Yet the very expression 'second-home problem' implies that such a problem exists and can be laid fully and unequivocally at the cottage door of second-home owners. If the second-home problem is defined as an external demand for housing leading to fewer affordable houses for those who must live in the countryside and hence to house-price inflation, then the effects of the retired and the commuter on house prices need to be examined carefully since such groups are often more numerous than second-home owners. The difficulty with housing policy is often an imprecise definition of which problems are being tackled and in what order of priority. If the problem is defined as the fact that some people own and occupy more houses than others, then this is really not a matter which any local planning authority ought to tackle directly since this principle is one on which only central government should legislate, if it so wishes. On the other hand, if the problem is seen as one of inadequate quality and quantity of housing for the lower paid in the countryside, then the sensible solution should be one addressed directly to the needs of that group. The fact that in Britain the planning authority can neither subsidise marginal house-buyers nor build houses for low-cost renting is a weakness of the planning system rather than a reason for employing land-use planning to alter the housing market.

Houses for purchase are not going to get much cheaper in real terms unless a great deal of new building takes place in an area. House prices are related to people's incomes in the long run and so, unless

there is a technical breakthrough which cheapens house construction
or a desire develops to live in houses the size of cupboards, outright
house ownership will always be beyond the reach of many with below
average incomes and wealth, and even partial ownership will be
expensive. Indeed there is clear evidence that the propensity to
spend more on housing as income rises is quite strong as people trade
up to houses with more rooms or larger gardens. Even though a house
is the largest purchase most people will ever make in their lives,
housing aspirations keep running ahead of income. Helping the poorer
sections buy a house can benefit the rest of the community but only
indirectly. The solution to the housing problems of the very poor has
to lie in an enhanced supply of cheap rented accommodation or raising
their incomes from employment or, failing that, from the social
security system. Where planning is concerned with the local community
as a group rather than the less well-off, discriminatory policies in
favour of the former have to be tempered by an awareness of the district's responsibilities to its region and the nation. The rest of
the country should not be allowed free rein, but it cannot be excluded
either. Planning must also ensure that, when acting to help the local
community against the rest of the state, it does not worsen the housing
prospect of its other charge, the less well-off.

Clearly there may be conflict between these two duties to the locality
and to the less well-off and planning can take steps to help both
groups. They can, for example, encourage self-build schemes. People
with the drive to build their own house are probably valuable in a
rural community. They bring in money, probably to local traders and
suppliers, and they are adding to the housing stock without any
commitment from public funds and without denying anyone else a house.
Local authorities might even wish to lease land they own to self-build
schemes to encourage this group who are likely to be permanent residents of considerable initiative.

Land-use planning can encourage the sub-division of existing houses
into flats and the conversion of other buildings so as to make more
intensive use of the existing housing stock without adding any more
buildings to the landscape. It can also smooth the path for employers
to provide accommodation for their staff. The many farmers who are
able to erect their own new farm steadings could well build a house
themselves for an example.

Planning can also alter the rate of new building or direct the inflow
of newcomers to one area or another. County towns can often accept
more residents without undue strain on local services or the landscape
and so could some rural areas where the farm work-force is shrinking
and is adequately housed already. Where the landscape is particularly
sensitive to new building and in those areas where housing need can be
detected among those already living there, speculative building could
be prohibited in the style of Danish rural planning but, in the
British context, without the need to pay compensation for restricting
development rights. This would avoid the need to try and defend a
blanket policy applied across a wide area which varies in its geography,
housing provision and scenic value. It is not reasonable to assume

that the externalities (both positive and negative) created by urban
pressures on rural housing markets are identical everywhere. Policy
should be operated in small areas where its validity can be checked
and where, if used well, its defence can be surer. However, the scope
of planning has to be recognised as limited. Planning can stop
developments where the disadvantages to the community are large but it
cannot by itself ensure houses are built where the social gains are
high. That task requires the close co-operation of planner and
housing authority and one would hope to see these links strengthened.

The features of rural planning which stand out most clearly from this
study are the fragmentation and conflicting objectives at scales
ranging from the local to the national. The fragmentation is exem-
plified at many different levels. For example, any system of local
planning needs administrative boundaries to separate one planning
authority from its neighbour but sometimes the countryside is broken
up into units which compound the planner's problems. To plan for
Dartmoor, Exmoor, the Peak District or the Lake District separately
from the neighbouring lowlands and towns cuts across the functional
unity of city and hinterland. This separates employment from work-
force and service centre from customers. The visual antithesis of town
and country belies their functional unity. Local government was so
divided in 1949 that there may have been merit then in such groupings
of rural areas to give a consistency of protection for the countryside.
Since the reorganisations of British local government in 1974 and 1975
which took more account of the 'city-region', the justification for
separate rural planning bodies has become questionable.

Fragmentation is also notable between planning and all other aspects
of local government which affect rural areas. The administrative
convenience in the past of separating planning from housing, transport
and education is obvious but this can be ossified into entrenched
departmental positions which impare co-ordinated action. Cloke, in
his study of key settlement policy, noted how an inability to co-
ordinate fully the different branches of local and national government
with the work of quangoes made for a less effectively implemented
policy than would otherwise have been the case (Cloke, 1979 pp.215-16).
Every government department and public body has a duty under Section
11 of the Countryside Act 1968 or Section 66 of the Countryside
(Scotland) Act of 1967 to 'have regard to the desirability of conservin
the natural beauty and amenity of the countryside.' The Countryside
Review Committee suggested that a broader duty should be imposed on
rural authorities to have regard to the socio-economic interests of the
countryside and its population but the Committee baulked at the problems of definition involved - that is, whose socio-economic interests
and whether long-term or short-term interests (1977, paras. 62-5).
The welfare and distributional effects of any proposed measure are as
important for decision makers as the aggregate effects even if esti-
mating distributional effects is difficult.

The Countryside Review Committee's other suggestion for more inte-
gration of policy required more co-ordination at national level betwee
departments. In Scotland there now exists a Standing Committee on Rur

Land Use which brings together the Department of Agriculture and Fisheries for Scotland, the Forestry Commission, the Scottish Development and Economic Planning Departments, the Nature Conservancy Council and the Countryside Commission for Scotland (Countryside Review Committee, 1976 para. 72 and D.A.F.S., 1977 p.29). Such groupings, whether loose associations or omnibus ministries of rural affairs as Wibberley (1976) has suggested, will only succeed in promoting balanced development so long as none of the interested parties is dominant. The suspicion is that in Whitehall generally and in the Countryside Review Committee in particular, the agricultural interest is still as dominant as it was at the time of the Scott Report in 1942. If this is the case, the administrative framework is of peripheral interest and it really does not matter greatly whether state forestry, for example, is controlled by a nominally independent body as in Great Britain or as a branch of the Department of Agriculture as in Northern Ireland. All these forms of organisation tend to be hidden behind veils of confidentiality so that it is often not possible to tell how rational or consistent is the decision making. This is, of course, a time-honoured feature of British administration which extends far beyond rural affairs.

It has also been suggested that planners and members of planning committees have a rather fragmented view of rural life which is a product of their training, the duties laid on them by the Planning Acts and the ethos of a planning profession where economics and sociology graduates, for example, are under-represented. This controversial view is the subject of current research to investigate whether it can be substantiated (Knox and Cullen, 1981). However, it is clear that consistency of decision making is particularly difficult in planning (Cloke, 1979 pp.214-15).

Another central feature of rural planning which emerges from a study of rural housing is that of conflict. This takes many forms, some of them obvious and others less so. Some divergence of interest exists between developer and conservationist, for example, farmer and recreationist, landlord and tenant. Much can be achieved to reduce conflict between individuals by informal discussion and compromise through worthwhile organisations such as the Lake District's Upland Management scheme. The Lake District's Section 52 policy has worked so well through just such discussion to persuade developers to accept the Board's aims. The system of planning inquiries offers a more formal and centralised system of arbitration. However, the unequal resources available to the parties at planning inquiries can generate suspicion of bias. The specific nature of planning inquiries - concern for a particular development at a particular place - can preclude broader discussions of whether a certain class of development is desirable. It is often difficult for objectors to prevent a specific development of a general type of which they disapprove, when the specific proposal is no better and no worse than many others like it. Nuclear power stations in rural areas are a case in point. Objectors often cannot use general arguments against all nuclear development to stop a specific proposal. The reverse situation is the difficulty for a planning authority to sustain a general policy introduced for broad socio-economic reasons when faced with a specific proposal for a small-scale development which is counter to its policy. One may be able to argue against any new houses in the Lake District, but the arguments are of a type unsuited to objecting convincingly to a proposal to build one house on a specified site.

Clearly the question of scale for the formulation and justification of rural planning policy is one whose importance has been under-valued. The areal extent of a policy - a building site, a village or a county - will mould the form of the arguments used to defend the policy. The planning system is being urged to widen its horizons and develop broader policies through structure plans. National Park authorities are required to take all such action as appears to them expedient to carry out the duties laid on them by the National Parks and Access to the Countryside Act of 1949, while Section 111 of the Local Government Act of 1972 reinforces this. Circular 4/76 from the Secretaries of State for the Environment and Wales endorsed the Sandford Committee's recommendation that the National Parks should aim to achieve wider social and economic objectives through their planning.

Yet the system of planning inquiries remains site specific and cannot easily incorporate large-area arguments of a socio-economic character. Thus there is a discontinuity of scale between policy formulation and arbitration of development proposals. There exists in theory the mechanism of the planning commission to bridge that gap but this device is rarely used - the Royal Commission on the Third London Airport was a cognate device and exceptional. This may be because investigation into the nuclear programme or housing policy, for example, takes local planning into territory properly reserved for the central departments of state. Yet a planning commission would conversely offer the local authority the stage on which to secure the broader style of planning being urged on it, but which the current system of planning inquiries renders so difficult to pursue.

Conflict, of course, can never be eliminated since land and houses are, by their nature immobile and limited both in quantity and specific qualities. There is only one Coniston Water, it is unique and, as a site for a lake-side house, few people will make do with Staines Reservoir even though this too is a body of standing water. Both land and house markets have implicit in them elements of potential monopoly because of their geographical distribution. This may be expressed in obvious fashion by large estates but monopoly can also exist within land and housing markets which have dispersed ownership, since both are highly differentiated in space and quality. The Lake District is one area where the substitution of another area of countryside for one's retirement home is often not acceptable and this enhances the inelasticity of demand for houses there.

Disagreements in rural planning not only exist over specific sites but also at a policy level since rural planning has been bedevilled by opposing objectives. This arises in part from differing interpretations of the problem to be solved. Poole (1970) noted the example of regional development policy in the Irish Republic where a lively debate occurred over whether over-population or emigration was the problem to be solved. The proponents of each of these definitions of the Irish regional problem differed in their preferred strategy for coping with the situation as they saw it. Similarly, ingrained aesthetic values on the role of forestry in the landscape may be so divergent for different groups that a consensus for landscape planning may be impossible. Other forms of conflict are inherent - Gilbert Fisher's paradox of providing solitude for the masses, for example, neatly summarises one conflict in recreational planning to which no solution would be possible in so small a country as Great Britain were it not for most people's tenacious attachment to their cars and the roads.

The transformation of most British rural areas noted in the recent results of the 1981 Population Census from regions of depopulation to ones of net inflow, raises the question of the appropriate planning policy for the countryside. It is an uncertainty made more poignant by the observation that when the countryside was depopulating, the aim was to bring more people into rural areas but it was never clear how to do this in more than in a few favoured places. The prospect now is of the countryside re-populating again, then a move to stop this and, pace the Section 52 policy, no conclusive method of achieving this being evident, permissible or fair.

Conflicting objectives also arise from the departmental structure of government. The Ministry of Agriculture is concerned with the farming interests of both the farmers and the nation while the Nature Conservancy Council is concerned with wildlife. If the extension of a more productive or profitable agriculture threatens wildlife or the visual character of an area, then the respective departments strive to have their interpretation prevail. The Porchester Inquiry into land use in Exmoor and the recent Countryside and Wildlife Act are clear cases of such conflicts within Government being worked out in specific cases. Conflicts could also arise from a change of government but in the British context the differences between Conservative and Labour parties in rural policy are not large. There are probably greater differences between the left and right wings of each party than between the party leaderships.

There is a need to examine critically the system of national parks, areas which, for planning purposes, are hived off to separate boards in the Lake and Peak Districts and to special committees of county councils elsewhere. If a fresh start were being made to the question of protecting the landscape and promoting recreation in the countryside, it is doubtful if the mechanism of national parks would be adopted. Selecting just ten areas of England and Wales for special treatment is a slight to the beauty of the rest of the countryside which does not deserve lesser protection. National parks boundaries tend to cut off upland areas from the lowlands with which they have such strong functional ties which makes planning very difficult. It is not easy to plan separately for one-half of an integrated system. In addition, the purpose of national parks is no longer as clear and distinctive as it once was. Separate administration invites separate treatment of

144

parks which are areas of great diversity separated from comparable
areas by boundaries of immense artificiality. Efficient, effective
control requires an ability to look at all the system's inputs and
outputs and the national park boundaries prevent that. The national
park function is a valuable one, though perhaps it could benefit from
some changes of emphasis. What is questionable is whether these
functions should be carried out by separate bodies called National
Parks rather than being part of the general system of local administration and planning which is implemented wherever needed.

Conflict of policy sometimes creates a stalemate and there is such
an administrative momentum to policy that it can take a long time to
alter a policy once it has started. It is always easier to start a
new policy than stop an old one. For example, it is easier to carry
on subsidising dairy production and then dispose of the surplus than
to stop the subsidy.

Policies may also conflict spatially in that they may be intended for
use in one area but then be applied more widely even when this is not
entirely appropriate. The policy of designating green belts is a case
in point. In the 1940s and 1950s this was arguably a useful tool for
stopping the inter-war expansion of London into the countryside. However, the power to create green belts was introduced nationally and
was used to restrict the growth of such small settlements as Stirling
(population 29,776 in 1971) and Prestwick Airport and to protect scrub
and semi-derelict land between Falkirk and Grangemouth (Skinner, 1976).
The use of policy measures introduced nationally for one area to
tackle, perhaps quite inappropriately, problems in other areas is quite
common in rural planning.

Conflict in rural planning can also arise from the inherent comp-
lexity of the countryside. Rural Britain is not just landscape or
farming. It is an amalgam of all that goes to make up modern life.
Consequently rural areas can be greatly altered by aspects of central
government policy which are far removed from a narrow definition of
planning. The most obvious case is fiscal policy. Taxes, such as
capital transfer tax, are used to generate revenue and to promote a
more equitable distribution of wealth, but the rate at which the tax
is levied presents difficulties for the countryside. If the rate of
tax is set too high - so meeting the revenue and equity objectives in
the short term - this may conflict with the long-term policy of
encouraging farmers to expand by amalgamation since farms may have to
be split to pay the tax. If, however, the tax is levied at a specially
low level for rural areas, it will fail to meet its fiscal objectives
and there may be an inflation of land and farm prices as urban people
seek to enter farming or own rural land to take advantage of the
concessions. This increased demand for farmland may so raise land
prices that farm expansion by real working farmers will be reduced,
farmers will be liable to capital taxation and the state forestry
programme will be made more expensive. Similarly, the tax on petrol
is used for revenue generation and to conserve oil stocks by reducing
consumption, but increasing this tax affects most severely those who
must travel long distances such as country people. It is not the

intention that this group should be more heavily taxed, but that is
the effect of the dominance of national monetary and fiscal policies
in rural affairs. The countryside is probably given little consideration in formulating the tax structure but the latter has a major and
distinctive effect on many aspects of businesses, employment and
housing markets.

Conflict also arises from the endemic failure of local and national
administration to grasp the essential inter-relatedness of rural life
and to so arrange the administrative framework that this inter-
relatedness is brought to the attention of the elected decision makers.
Consider, for example, housing, transport and services. Each is the
concern of a different department at local and national level, yet
each influences the others. Where people live and the location of the
facilities they wish to use will affect the transport arrangements
which must be provided for those who need public transport. Conversely,
changes in the provision of public transport may affect patronage of
shops or where people work. A policy to centralise schools, for
example, may reduce some obvious public costs such as teacher's
salaries and building maintenance, but it will also increase the cost
of transporting pupils to the schools, a factor which is often not
considered fully when deciding on the location of schools. The concentration of health facilities in fewer hospitals may save the health
authority money but cost patients and visitors dearly for extra
travel. The location of factories may influence where people wish to
live and how far they have to commute but such control as there is
over the siting of factories does not concern itself with such matters.
Decisions on public transport will affect land use or at least affect
the demands placed on land-use planners. When key settlement policy
attempted some form of unified approach to housing, transport and
services, its implementation was, for good or ill, often imperfect
due in part to the fragmented and poorly co-ordinated nature of
planning in its broadest sense.

Rural planning is also notable for the predominant influence of
agricultural considerations at all levels of administration. Farmers'
incomes have been subsidised, their investments have been grant-aided
and most agricultural changes have been automatically approved under
the General Development Order. Such a predominant position for one
land use and one section of the rural community is not necessarily
healthy. Recently there have been moves to exert greater control over
farming and this has been one symptom of the rise of another predominant facet of planning, namely landscape protection. While this
too is important - though much less so than food production - it can
be pursued with a single-mindedness which is not conducive to well-
balanced rural planning. A 'best development is no development'
approach not only allows no change and thereby lessens the chance of
improvement but it will exhibit in extreme form that inflation of land
prices which Hall attributes to land-use planning generally in Britain
since 1947 (Hall, 1974b).

It is not clear for whom local planning should be carried out. Should
it be for the local area or the nation? Excessive concern for local

needs can create a dykes mentality seeking to repel incomers, which is
not acceptable within a nation state and is questionable even for
self-governing areas such as the Channel Islands. Recourse to
planning solely in the national interest is not only electorally
unpopular with local politicians but also opens up the nebulous concept
of the 'national interest' and dangerously saps local initiative. The
danger with the post-Sandford policy for the national parks is that it
may veer excessively to a definition of the national interest based on
the preservation of the landscape and thereby reduce development and
promote depopulation and socio-economically unbalanced communities.
Rural planning needs to tread the narrow path between excessive
parochialism and the submergence of local needs by national interest.
Planning should mould development not stiffle it and should reduce the
negative externalities of development. In housing these objectives
could best be met by operating housing policy as far down as the parish
level.

Rural planning should also be designed to help those who are unable
to enjoy an average standard of living. Like the subsidised provision
of council housing it should try to mitigate the harsher, more
regressive effects of the free market and laisser-faire. This is
particularly important in rural areas because, while no one has any
more right to live in Coniston or Grasmere than in Mayfair, the
alternative rural jobs or houses are fewer and more scattered. The
fundamental rural character of low density is a sufficient condition
to require a spatially sensitive form of planning which is different
from the city and this could be implemented with help from enhanced
parish and community councils and councils of social service, a point
of which even the Treasury approve (Treasury 1976 p.25).

Do planners and their political masters know what kind of countryside
they want in the year 2000? Probably they do not, since this would
require a consensus on matters such as the extent of state intervention, the relative importance of farming and landscape protection
and the relative importance of private enterprise, planning and public
provision in shaping this future geography. Such a consensus would be
difficult, perhaps unlikely even, yet a Royal Commission should clarify
the questions and the options in an area of limited dispute between the
major political parties. Such long-term planning - guidelines for
central government policy might be a better term - would be a valuable
counterweight to the superficiality of structure planning and the vital
but inevitably day-to-day tasks of development control. In specific
terms, whether the Lake District and the other national parks should
become deserts with gift shops or Eastbourne with mountains is highly
relevant to the way local planning is used.

If we need a new Scott Report to debate these issues and publish its
arguments, then we also need to allow as much local initiative as
possible to be displayed, provided this does not usurp national policy
or financial guidelines which must set the ultimate constraints for
housing policy. In that sense, the Section 52 policy in the Lake
District was exactly the sort of innovative approach which should be
tried by local planning and housing authorities.

The future of rural planning now looks less certain than at any time in the last thirty years. The old certainties about rural life, perhaps they were really misunderstandings, have been discredited. What is left are areas different from the cities to be sure, but subject increasingly to the same attitudes, values and institutions as the cities.

'The same line of reasoning that leads to the expectation that the city will diffuse itself until it has taken up considerable areas and many of the characteristics, the greenness, the fresh air, of what is now country, leads us to suppose also that the country will take to itself many of the qualities of the cities. The old antithesis will indeed cease, the boundary lines will altogether disappear; it will become indeed, merely a question of more or less populous.'

(Wells, 1914 pp.63-4).

It is unlikely that change will come quickly. There are signs of a realisation that rural planning needs to be better integrated at local and national level with cognate branches of administration of which housing is the most obvious. The difficulty of turning back the urban tide is appreciated more widely than before while the position of agriculture and forestry outside planning control is being perceptibly eroded. Confidence in the ability of planning to do good is not as high as previously which may be unfair but is perhaps inevitable in a profession whose main achievements have been preventing undesirable developments. In addition to being able to say that the present and the future would have been worse without planning, one would like to see planning proposing a better future. Sadly there is very little sign that there is much concerted thought on what form that better future might take or on the type of planning (if any) needed to achieve it.

Postscript

Rural housing in the Lake District has evolved since the previous chapters were written. By 1981, housebuilding in Cumbria was 31 per cent above the Structure Plan target, despite the reduction nationally in the rate of house building (C.C.C. and L.D.S.P.B., 1981). Population has grown at a rate nearer that forecast in the Joint Structure Plan than in the estimates given by the Office of Population Censuses and Surveys. The number of substandard houses in Cumbria is thought to have fallen from 26,021 in 1971 to about 13,363 in 1980 but 18 per cent of the county's housing stock is still believed to be unfit, substandard or in need of major renovation. Improvement grants are available at only a quarter of the rate in the early to mid-1970s and housing allocations by the six Cumbria district councils in 1981-2 were 16 per cent lower than in 1980-1.

By late 1980, the number of Section 52 agreements had risen to 308 with 51 more houses subject to local person conditions. In mid-1980, 39 out of 227 Section 52 and 'local person' houses had been completed with a further 24 under construction. However, the future of such Section 52 agreements remains in doubt. The Secretary of State's intention to remove the local person restriction on new housing from the Joint Structure Plan has been challenged by the Planning Board with strong support from local Members of Parliament and there is some optimism that the policy will survive. In the event of the policy being removed however, the Planning Board are preparing other ways of achieving their objective of helping local people to obtain housing. Equity purchase schemes with a housing association and low-cost partnership schemes appear the most promising tactics, particularly where the land is already owned by the Planning Board. The shortage of funds persists for traditional council housing and housing association developments for renting in the Lake District.

January 1982

Cumbria County Council and Lake District Special Planning Board (1981) Progress 81 - Annual Monitoring Report, 1980-81.

Bibliography

Bennett, S. (1976). Rural Housing in the Lake District. University of Lancaster.

Blythe, R. (1969). Akenfield. Penguin, Harmondsworth.

Boddy, M. (1980). The Building Societies. Macmillan, London.

Burke, G. (1981). Housing and Social Justice. Longman, London.

Burnett, J. (1978). A Social History of Housing, 1815-1970. David and Charles, Newton Abbot.

Buttler, F.A. (1975). Growth Pole Theory and Economic Development. Saxon House, Farnborough.

Capstick, M. (1972). Some Aspects of the Economic Effects of Tourism in Westmorland Lake District, University of Lancaster.

Census Research Unit (1980). People in Britain - a Census Atlas, H.M.S.O.

Clark, G. (forthcoming). How many second homes in the Lake District?

Cloke, P. (1979). Key Settlements in Rural Areas. Methuen, London.

Clout, H. (1972). Rural Geography: an Introductory Survey. Pergamon, Oxford.

Cobbett, W. (1967). Rural Rides. vol. 2, Everyman, London.

Comhairle nan Eilean (1976). Regional Report.

Cosgrove, D.E. (1979). John Ruskin and the geographical imagination. Geographical Review 69, 43-62.

Coull, J.R. (1968). Crofters' Common Grazings in Scotland. Agricultural History Review 16, 142-54.

Countryside Review Committee (1976). The Countryside - Problems and Policies. H.M.S.O.

Countryside Review Committee (1977). Rural Communities. H.M.S.O.

Cullingworth, J.B. (1979). Essays on Housing Policy - the British Scene. Allen and Unwin, London.

Cumbria County Council and Lake District Special Planning Board (1976). Choices for Cumbria - Structure Plan, Report of Survey.

Cumbria County Council and Lake District Special Planning Board (1980). Joint Structure Plan - Written Statement.

152

Department of Agriculture and Fisheries for Scotland (D.A.F.S.) (1976). Leaflet CG8.

Department of Agriculture and Fisheries for Scotland (D.A.F.S.) (1977). Agriculture in Scotland - Report for 1976. Cmnd 6756, H.M.S.O.

Department of Agriculture and Fisheries for Scotland (D.A.F.S.) (1980). Agriculture in Scotland - Report for 1979. Cmnd 7870, H.M.S.O.

Department of the Environment (1974). Report of the National Park Policies Review Committee. H.M.S.O.

Department of the Environment (1976). Report of the National Park Policies Review Committee - Statement of the Conclusions of the Secretaries of State for the Environment and Wales on the Report. Circular 4/76.

Dunn, M.C.; M.J.C. Rawson and A.W. Rogers (1980). The Derivation of Rural Housing Profiles. Research Memorandum 76, Centre for Urban and Regional Studies, Birmingham.

Dunn, M.C; M.J.C. Rawson and A.W. Rogers (1981). Rural Housing: Competition and Choice. Allen and Unwin, London.

Edwards, J.A. (1971). The Viability of Lower Size-Order Settlements in Rural Areas: the case of North-East England. Sociologia Ruralis 11, 247-76.

Engels, F. (1892). The Condition of the Working Class in England in 1844. Allen and Unwin, London.

Evans, D.M. (1981). Key Settlement Policy - an Inappropriate Approach for Pressured Rural Areas. I.B.G. Conference Paper, Leicester.

Fletcher, P. (1975). The Agricultural Housing Problem. pp. 173-9 in Agriculture D203III, Open University, Milton Keynes.

Frankland, M. (1966). Khrushchev. Penguin, Harmondsworth.

Gasson, R. (1975). Provision of Tied Cottages. Occasional Paper 4, Department of Land Economy, University of Cambridge.

Gilder, I.M. (1979). Rural planning policies: an economic appraisal. Progress in Planning 11, 213-71.

Gilg, A.W. (1978). Countryside Planning: the First Three Decades, 1945-76. Methuen, London.

Gray, F. and M. Boddy (1979). The origins and use of theory in urban geography - household mobility and filtering theory. Geoforum 10, 117-27.

Hall, P. (1974a). Urban and Regional Planning. Penguin, Harmondsworth.

Hall, P. (1974b). The containment of urban England. Geographical Journal 140, 386-417.

Headey, B. (1978). Housing Policy in the Developed Economy. Croom Helm, London.

Holmes, M. (1973). Slices of Danish Land. Geographical Magazine 45(11), 772-4.

House of Commons Environment Committee (1980). Minutes of evidence on council house sales from Allerdale District Council and South Lakeland District Council. Session 1979-80, H.C.P. 535 iii.

Howard, E. (1946). Garden Cities of To-morrow. Faber and Faber, London.

Isle of Man Government (1980). Isle of Man Digest of Economic and Social Statistics.

Johnson, S. (1971). A Journey to the Western Islands of Scotland. Yale University Press, New Haven.

Knox, P. and J. Cullen (1981). Town planning and the internal survival mechanisms of urbanised capitalism. Area 13(3), 183-8.

Lake District Special Planning Board (1978). Lake District National Park Plan.

Lake District Special Planning Board (1979). Development Control Committee Minutes, July 1979.

Lake District Special Planning Board (1980). Supplementary Evidence to the Examination in Public of the Joint Structure Plan.

Larkin, A. (1978). Rural housing: too dear, too far, too few. Roof, January 1978.

Larkin, A. (1979). Rural Housing and Housing Need, in J.M. Shaw Rural Deprivation and Planning. Geo Books, Norwich.

Lowenthal, D. and H. Prince (1965). English landscape tastes. Geographical Review 55, 186-222.

Mather, A.S. (1978). State-Aided Land Settlement in Scotland. O'Dell Memorial Monograph No. 6, Department of Geography,

154

University of Aberdeen.

Millman, R. (1970). The landed properties of northern Scotland. Scottish Geographical Magazine 86(3), 186-203.

Ministry of Works and Planning (1942). Report of the Committee on Land Utilisation in Rural Areas. (The Scott Report) Cmd 6378, H.M.S.O.

Morris, H. (1925). The Village College. Cambridge University Press, Cambridge. (Reprinted in full in Ree, H. (1973) q.v.).

Moseley, M.J. (1973). Growth centres - a shibboleth? Area 5(2), 143-50.

National House Builders Federation (1980). Evidence to the Examination in Public of the Joint Structure Plan. Kendal.

Newby, H. (1977). The Deferential Worker. Allen Lane, London.

Newby, H. (ed.) (1978). International Perspectives on Rural Sociology. Wiley, Chichester.

Pallot, J. (1979). Rural Settlement Planning in the Soviet Union, Soviet Studies 31(2), 214-30.

Parsons, D.J. (1977). Rural Settlement and Land Use Planning. Rural Geography Study Group Conference Paper, Lancaster.

Parsons, D.J. (n.d.). Rural Gentrification: the Influence of Rural Settlement Planning Policies. Research Paper in Geography, University of Sussex.

Peake, H. (1922). The English Village. Benn, London.

Perroux, F. (1950). Economic space: theory and applications. Quarterly Journal of Economics 64, 89-104.

Poole, M.A. (1970). Decision Making and the Formulation of Regional Development Objectives: the Case of Rural Ireland. Irish Geographical Studies 312-24.

Ree, H. (1973). Educator Extraordinary - the Life and Achievement of Henry Morris, 1889-1961. Longman, London.

Rogers, A.W. (1976). Rural Housing, in G.E. Cherry (ed.) Rural Planning Problems. Leonard Hill, London.

Rogers, A.W. (1981). Housing in the National Parks. Town and Country Planning July/August 1981, 193-5.

Ryle, G. (1969). Forest Service. David and Charles, Newton Abbot.

Sandbach, F.E. (1978). The early campaign for a National Park in the Lake District. Transactions of the Institute of British Geographers (New Series) 3(4), 498-514.

Shucksmith, D.M. (1980). Evidence to the Examination in Public of the Joint Structure Plan. Kendal.

Shucksmith, D.M. (1981). No Homes for Locals? Gower, Farnborough.

Skinner, D.N. (1976). A Situation Report on Green Belts in Scotland. Occasional Paper 8, Countryside Commission for Scotland.

Smith, F.V. (1976). Sociological Survey of Border Forest Villages, Forestry Commission Research and Development Paper No. 112.

Symonds, H.H. (1936). Afforestation in the Lake District. Dent, London.

The Government's Expenditure Plans, 1980-1 to 1983-84. (1980). Cmnd 7841, H.M.S.O.

Thompson, F. (1945). Lark Rise to Candleford. Oxford University Press, Oxford.

Thormodsaeter, A. (1965). Land Use Planning in Mountain Areas of Norway. Proceedings of the first Scandinavian - Polish Regional Science seminar, Szczecin, 71-83.

Town and Country Planning Act 1971 ch. 78, Town and Country Planning Act 1947 ch. 51, s14(1) and Fawcett Properties Ltd. v Buckingham County Council, 1960, All England Law Reports 1960(3), 503-28.

Treasury, H.M. (1976). Rural Depopulation. H.M.S.O.

Vane, R. de (1975). Second Home Ownership. University of Wales Press, Cardiff.

Wagstaff, H.R. (1973). Employment multipliers in rural Scotland. Scottish Journal of Political Economy 20, 239-61.

Wells, H.G. (1914). Anticipations Chapman and Hall, London.

Whittington, G. (forthcoming). Agriculture and Society in Lowland Scotland, 1750-1870, in G. Whittington and I.D. Whyte (eds) An Historical Geography of Scotland. Academic Press, London.

Whyte, I.D. (1979). Agriculture and Society in Seventeenth Century Scotland. John Donald, Edinburgh.

Wibberley, G. (1976). Rural resource development in Britain and environmental concern. Journal of Agricultural Economics 27, 1-18.

Wordsworth, W. (1835). Guide to the Lakes. Fifth edition reprinted
in 1925 by Humphrey Milford, London.

Index

Agriculture Act (1970), 31
Agrotown, 42
'Akenfield', 14
Agricultural depression, 11,
  12-14, 40
Agricultural Dwelling House
  Advisory Committee, 38
Argyllshire, 14
Bedford, Duke of, 10
Bondager, 6
Bothies, 6, 30
Building costs, 20 see also
  Lake District
Building societies, 1, 104-5,
  121, 130-1
Cambridgeshire, 40
Canada, 120
Channel Islands, 97, 123-6, 146
Chaumer, 5
Closed villages, 29
Cobbett, William, 8, 12
Commuting, 21
Cornwall, 25
Council houses (United Kingdom)
  19, 26 see also Lake District
Crown Estate Commissioners, 37
Cumberland, 40, 45, 51 see also
  Lake District
Denmark,
  land-use zoning, 112
  smallholdings, 16
Dennison, S.R., 24
Department of the Environment,
  96
Development Commission, 46
Devon, 36, 45
Dumfriesshire, 32
Durham, 45
East Anglia, 20, 25
Electricity supply, 22
Enclosure Commissioners, 11
Engels, Friedrich, 6
England,
  eastern, 36
  north-east, 14-16
  northern, 5
  south-west, 20
First World War, 14, 30
Forestry Commission, 14-16, 55-7
Forestry villages, 14-16

Garden City, 11-12
Glasgow, 11, 126
Great Barrington, 29
Great Tew, 29
Gretna, 19
Growth pole theory, 44
Guernsey see Channel Islands
Hebrides, 6-7 see also Western
  Isles
Hinds, 6
House Condition Survey (1976),
  25
Housing Acts,
  Housing Acts, 1890 to 1909,
    11, 18
  Housing, Town Planning etc.
    Act, 1919, 18-19
  Housing etc. Act, 1923, 19
  Housing (Financial
    Provisions) Act, 1924, 19
  Housing (Financial
    Provisions) Act, 1938, 19
Housing Associations, 127-8
Howard, Ebenezer, 11-12
Hutterites, 12
Industry, 23-4, 40-2 see also
  Lake District
Interdepartmental Committee on
  Agricultural Tied Cottages
  (1932), 32
Ireland, 6
Isle of Man, 120-3, 130
Jersey see Channel Islands
Johnson, Samuel, 6-7
Key settlements, 39-47
  Soviet Union, 42-3
Labour Commission (1892-4), 8
Labour Party, 22, 30, 37, 126
Lake District, 49-110, 132-4
  activity rates, 60-3
  climate, 51
  common land, 53
  cost of living, 60-3
  council housing, 60-81, 96
    99, 107-9
    demand for, 60-7
    waiting list for, 64-73
  depopulation, 85
  employment structure, 60,
    85-8

establishment of National
Park, 57
Friends of the Lake District,
55
Hardknott Estate, 55
house prices, 83, 88, 98-9,
101-5, 107-8
housing associations, 53, 73,
127-8
housing need, 75-81
housing quality, 75, 83
incomes, 60-2
Keswick, 51, 64, 67
Lake District (Special)
Planning Board, 57-60, 83,
88-98, 107, 109
landownership, 53
landscape, 51-3, 60, 88-91,
96, 108
local person condition, 96,
105
Lowther Estates, 53
National Trust, 53
North West Water Authority, 53
population structure, 85
relief, 51
second homes, 88, 97
Section 52 policy, 96-110,
112-4,
assessment of, 98-107
implications of, 107-110
unemployment, 55, 63
Upland Management Scheme, 141
Windermere, 51, 83, 88
Lancashire, 27, 32
Landscape beauty, 23-4, 27, 41
see also Lake District
Leicestershire, 8, 40, 46
Letchworth (Herts), 12
licensee, 31
Liverpool, 11
Lloyd George, David, 16
London, 11, 12, 19
Loss of farm land, 23-5
Mennonites, 12
Miasma, 9
Migration to cities, 10-12, 21,
23, 39-40
Ministry of Health, 22, 41-2

Ministry of Town and Country
Planning, 42
Mormons, 12
National Coal Board, 30
National Farmers Union, 35, 38
National Land and Home League,
18
National Parks, 27
Lake District National Park,
49-110, 128-35
National Union of Agricultural
and Allied Workers, 36-9
Netherlands,
East Flevoland polder, 44
Newcastle, Duke of, 10
Norfolk, 42, 46
Northumberland, 14
Norway,
land-use zoning, 111-12
smallholdings, 16
Nottinghamshire, 46
Orkney, 7
Owen, Robert, 11
Oxfordshire, 29-30
Parker-Morris standards, 128
Peak District, 25
Police, 11
Poor Law, 10, 29-30
Port Sunlight, 30
Rent Acts, 31
Rent (Agriculture) Act 1965,
31
Rent (Agriculture) Act 1976,
37, 39
Rent Restrictions Acts, 21,
34
Rosyth Dockyard, 19
Rowntree, Joseph, 10
Sandford Report, 96, 142
Scotland,
central, 32, 44
east-central, 6
north-east, 6, 25
south-east, 5-6
south-west, 14
southern, 32
Scott Report (1942), 21-5,
32-5, 40-1, 146 see also
Dennison, S.R.

Scottish Housing Advisory
  Committee, 20
Scottish Special Housing
  Association, 126-7
Second homes, 21-3 see also
  Lake District
Second World War, 20
Service tenant, 31
Sewage works, 42-3, 45
Shakers, 12
Smallholdings,
  Denmark, 16
  Finland, 16
  Norway, 16
  United Kingdom, 16-18
Social polarisation, 46
Somerset, 40
Spain, 44
Stock Exchange, 20
Suffolk, 43
Tacksmen, 7
Tenants-at-will, 6
Tied accommodation, 21, 29-39,
  130
  distribution of, 32-4
  origins of, 29-30
  legal position, 30-1
  Scott Report on, 32-5
Trades union, 20
Transport and General Workers
  Union, 36
Union Chargeability Act (1865),
  10
Village colleges, 40
Wages (farm workers) 14, 20-3,
  34, 40 see also Lake District
Wales, 14, 20, 25, 32
  central, 14
  north, 27
Warnford Charter, 38
Warwickshire, 45
water supply, 14, 21-2, 45
Welwyn Garden City, 12
West Germany, 18, 120
Western Isles, 18, 114-120,
  130
Woolwich Arsenal, 19
Wordsworth, William, 24, 51,
  57
Yorkshire, 32